So, Ye Want To Be A Reenactor?

A Living History Handbook

—〜〜〜—

Brenton C. Kemmer & Karen L. Kemmer

HERITAGE BOOKS, INC.

Cover Photo by Ron Casto

Other Heritage Books by Brenton C. Kemmer:

*Freemen, Freeholders and Citizen Soldiers: An Organizational
History of Colonel Jonathan Bagley's Regiment, 1755-1760*

*Redcoats, Yankee and Allies: A History of the Uniforms,
Clothing and Gear of the British Army in the
Lake George-Lake Champlain Corridor, 1755-1760*

Published 2001 by

HERITAGE BOOKS, INC.
1540E Pointer Ridge Place
Bowie, Maryland 20716
1-800-398-7709
www.heritagebooks.com

ISBN 0-7884-1732-0

This book is a family-friendly introduction to the world of living history. The Kemmers take a common sense approach to getting started in reenacting and bridge the gap between veteran reenactors and the general reader. Best of all, they enthusiastically share their passion for the hobby and give advice that will help aspiring reenactors avoid some common pitfalls.
—Robert Emerson, Executive Director, Old Fort Niagara.

A clear and orderly approach to reenacting marks this book as one that will prove useful throughout the years for many people who are looking for some helpful hints to get started in this hobby.
—Harry & Rose Burgess, professional educators.

Reenacting is more than the proper clothes; it is responsibility, friendship, and fun. Brent and Karen bring the reader into this world of time travel. —Andrew Gallup, author.

If you think that you are interested in taking up the hobby of reenacting, then this book might be your best next step. It is full of information and stories that can save you both time and money as you start down your own trail of reenacting adventures. Brent and Karen Kemmer have a passion for reenacting and have learned much during their years in this hobby. So whether you are just new to reenacting or have been participating for years, I am sure you will learn from the experiences the Kemmers share in this book. —Jeff Dykehouse, Interpretation Supervisor, Mackinac State Historic Parks.

This book is a welcome resource for fledgling reenactors, and a trip down memory lane for grizzled veterans. —Tim Todish, author, Suagothel Productions, Ltd., Grand Rapids, Michigan.

Through their personal anecdotes, stories, and own experience, authors Brent and Karen Kemmer provide a valuable, comprehensive resource guide which should be most helpful to the beginning reenactor or anyone considering entering into the living history hobby. Professional and amateur historians, historic site managers and museum directors as well as veteran reenactors will also certainly be able to relate to their own topics associated with the living history hobby and historical interpretation. —Dr. Todd E. Harburn, author, The Michilimackinac Society Press, Lansing Michigan.

✍ Contents ✍

—✂✂✂✂✂✂—

⚘ Preface ⚘

———✽———

Looking around the encampment at a living history event this past season, my wife, Karen, came up with the idea for this book. We had strived to set up this encampment as authentically as possible, and it was really coming together beautifully. Karen was reminiscing about how we had first gotten started in reenacting many years ago, and all the adventures we had experienced since then. We had come a long way.

After we got home and had settled back into our weekly routine, we talked in-depth about her ideas and the possibility of co-authoring a book based on our respective reenacting experiences. For years Karen had wanted to write a book, and now that our son, Brent II, was departing for his first year at college, the timing seemed right for this project.

If you are interested in getting involved in this hobby, you should:
* love doing research,
* love camping,
* love talking to people,
* have a passion for history and
* know what you're doing before you make or buy anything.

We are not the all-knowing experts or the "authenticity police." We do have some qualifications and MANY experiences and ideas to pass along to you. Karen graduated with a B.S. degree in history and political science in 1977. In 1990, she earned a teaching certificate and since then has furthered her graduate studies with an additional endorsement. In 1988 I received my B.S. degrees in history and biology with a concentration in museum science and a teaching certificate. Then in 1994, I received an M.A. specializing in early American history. We have twenty years of living history-reenactor experience in ten different organizations and have started our own successful living history organization with members from over 35 families and four states. We also have taken part in a feature length movie, have been extras in several A&E and History Channel specials and have authored many articles and several historical non-fiction books. All of this in no way is meant to brag, exaggerate or set us apart from other living historians, but solely to let you know our backgrounds and interests as they relate to our hobby.

The best ways for us to share our ideas with you is through examples and stories of some of our personal experiences. You will quickly notice our bias toward the Seven Years' War (French and Indian War). We portray Colonel Jonathan Bagley's 3rd Massachusetts Regiment, Co. C. Because of this you can expect many of our examples to be of this era.

◄◆►

KAREN: The way we got started in living history makes a good story to begin this book with. Shortly before our son was born, Brent thought it would be a great idea to have a gun to hang above the fireplace mantel of our apartment. (He's into decorating, after working for several years in a designer furniture store.) One of my friends and I were Christmas shopping at a department store and ran across Kentucky rifle kits for fifty dollars! Her husband, Bill, worked with Brent, and so she and I decided to buy the rifle kits for our husbands for the holidays. "The boys" worked all winter putting together their kits. (Brent worked on his in the living room with a knife, razorblade-knife and sandpaper.)

Finally, in the spring the rifles were complete and one of the men came up with the idea to take them to a shoot and see how well they worked. Brent and Bill did quite well in competitions that summer, often placing 5th and 6th. Then at one shoot they saw several guys dressed in "costumes" (I hate the word). Since Brent's favorite movie at that time was "The Mountain Men," he ran home and called his dad, who gave him all the old deerskins he had kept over the years. Brent made himself a pair of fringed buckskin trousers. He also took an old cowboy hat and punched the crown up and pulled down the brim, forming a crude round hat blank. Then, of course he had me make him a muslin shirt from instructions in "The Book of Buckskinning II." That really got Brent going, for shortly afterward he decided he needed to be more authentic to the history of our state, Michigan, so we made him some French colonial period clothing. Brent II and I soon got into the act when I made period clothing for us as well. I guess I would have to blame myself for our passion in living history.

We hope this book will inspire new participants in this hobby we call living history or reenacting. We also hope that those who are already enjoying this hobby will find the book interesting and helpful in their continual quest for perfection. Finally, we hope that historic interpreters, historic sites and professional living historians can glean some information from our experiences and ideas.

Brent Kemmer
Karen Kemmer

"Has anyone seen my leeches?" Here surgeon Caleb Rea (AKA Joe Lee) sets up his equipment for public demonstration at a living history event. Props make excellent icebreakers with the public. Photo by Brent Kemmer.

✤ 1 ✤

What Is "Living History?"

—✒✒✿✒✒—

Living history is the simulation of people, events, places or situations as they existed in some past time. By experiencing and demonstrating the activities, sights, sounds, smells and flavors of the past, living historians increase their own understanding as they educate others and stimulate our interest in history.

When we think of living history, most of us think of soldiers in tri-cornered hats or frontier-types in buckskins, but there is much more to it than that. Living history may be the single best way to convey our human heritage to others. This form of education is stimulating to the intellect, and its interactive qualities encourage others to become personally involved with the study of our past.

Living history is not a new technique, but rather a time-tested tool utilized for decades by professionals and amateurs alike. Places like Colonial Williamsburg, Conner's Prairie and Plymouth Plantation have successfully employed living history programs for many years, and can be considered among the leaders of this form of historical interpretation.

Many of us would like to see a more enthusiastic patriotic spirit among our young people and fellow Americans. Living history is a unique way to spark people's desire to become more knowledgeable as to our global, national, state and local histories, and to inspire future generations with a passion for history.

Fig. 1. "Rope line work" as we call it is a good form of interpretation. It not only shares information with visitors but also allows them to interact with reenactors and living historians in a very comfortable manner.

Living history can be separated into three areas of study: Interpreting, Reenacting, and Experimental Archaeology.

✑ INTERPRETING

> *Interpretation is an educational activity which aims to reveal meanings and relationships through the use of original objects, by firsthand experience, and by illustrative media, rather than simply to communicate factual information.[1]*

Many professional living historians consider Freeman Tilden the guru of interpreting. His ideas and ideals of education are fundamental to all professional and amateur living historians. His book, *Interpreting Our Heritage*, epitomizes our form of educating.

Many of us who interpret the Colonial period practice "rope line work." Many of our camps are set up with a rope line around it. This rope line serves several purposes. First, it keeps the public away from fire pits and weapons, and any other objects that might cause injury. Second, the rope line works as a minimum barrier, separating, in our case, the 18th century from the 21st.

A friend of ours, who portrays an 18th-century sailor attached to the colonial militia, is a good example of a rope line interpreter. He spreads out a blanket on the ground in front of his tent and empties the contents of his ditty bag onto it. Then he explains to passing visitors what the items are and how they were used in the day-to-day life of a sailor.

Interpretation can take on many forms depending on which time period you choose to portray, your form (1st, 2nd, or 3rd person) and depth of living history, level of knowledge of the period, and whether you're working professionally or as an amateur.

---

[1] Freeman Tilden, *Interpreting Our Heritage* (Chapel Hill, NC: University of North Carolina Press) 8.

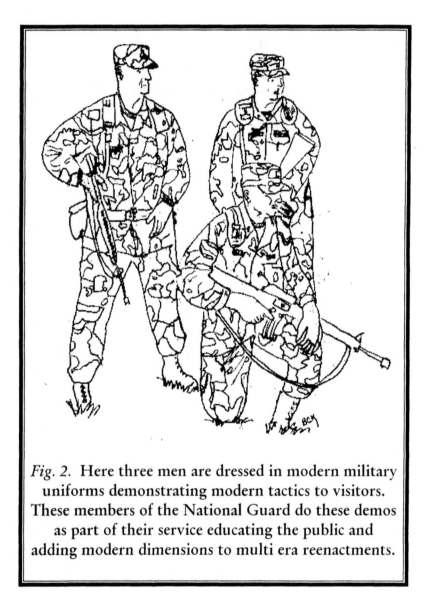

Fig. 2. Here three men are dressed in modern military uniforms demonstrating modern tactics to visitors. These members of the National Guard do these demos as part of their service educating the public and adding modern dimensions to multi era reenactments.

Fig. 3. This father and son have refurbished a WWII jeep and collected surplus uniforms and gear for a once a year chance to educate their local community about one of our nation's involvements in a global conflict.

Several historic sites have produced their own training manuals and videos to help living historians enhance and develop programs for the public. These instructional materials cover everything from clothing to speech patterns. Interpretation does not necessarily require historic clothing either, although that is our passion and what the majority of this book will deal with. Museums, historical societies and historic sites often have exhibits with written information for self-interpretation. These organizations often also have docents (guides) on site to talk to, lead and enthuse visitors. This is the basic form of site interpretation. Traditionally this has met the needs of most visitors.

With the never-ending quest to enhance educational techniques, many sites have developed costumed living history programs. This approach has flourished and encompasses all areas and time periods of our national history. Such programs range from simple costumed informational docents leading tours to first person interpretation.

BRENT: Here is an example of how this type of living history can be used to enhance the quality of a visitor's experience at a museum. While working at The Museum of Cultural and Natural History at Central Michigan University I took part in the development of a living history program. When a group was scheduled to tour the museum, I would dress in period clothing and take my place in the museum galley near an exhibit of the same period. Docents would lead groups through the gallery, giving them general information on exhibits. When they got to me, I would be introduced and would take over at that point, explaining to the visitors about the time period, artifacts and exhibit. This method of visitor interaction became very successful and eventually I talked our director into letting me remove the glass on our 1700's fur trade post exhibit. I would then get into the exhibit and more realistically talk in first person to the visitors from a more believable setting. I must stress though, this method works best with a docent leading the tour so that if there are children, especially school groups, the docent can remove problem children so the historical interpreter doesn't have to break character to deal with the misbehavers.

Within a year, we developed five historic characters for visitors to request, depending on their group's specific interest. Each character was portrayed by a trained interpreter in reproduction period clothing and with real and reproduction artifacts to stimulate our talks. When it was time for me to move on, the director asked me to make a video to train new interpreters to the museum. This training video is still in use today.

A MOST MEMORABLE VISIT

At the other extreme are sites like Plymouth Plantation. This is the best-interpreted site we ever visited! These interpreters *are* the people who came from England in 1620! Their first person presentations are superb. When we visited, it was a rainy day, but we were determined to make a go of it.

We spent a lot of time in the buildings conversing with the interpreters, but one, Governor Winthrop, really showed us true first person interpretation at the highest level. Karen and I were both in his house. Karen was watching Winthrop's wife tend the fire, and I was standing in the background observing everything I could while the governor was talking with others. Winthrop finished talking and the other people moved on, so I stepped closer and started to peer intently at all the reproduction glassware, furniture and other artifacts near and around the table where he sat. To my left was a small bookshelf on the wall, and, being very self-indulgent when it comes to historic books, I asked if he minded if I looked at them. He gave his permission, so I took down a book and started thumbing through it with great interest. Meanwhile, Karen had walked back across the room and had placed herself behind me. She reached over my shoulder and pointed out and read an interesting sentence to me. No sooner had she stopped than Winthrop stated, "I see you've taught your lady to read." We were both taken in awe with his skill at placing all

"Colonel Bagley" (Brent) narrates as a group of French and Indian War soldiers demonstrate the proper usage of their weapons to visitors at Fort William Henry, Lake George, NY. Photo by Karen Kemmer.

"Cover your ears!" At many forts, reenactors are a vital source of interpretation for the public. This unit of Massachusetts soldiers of the 1750's fires a volley for onlookers at Colonial Michilimackinac, Mackinaw City, MI. Photo by Beth Ignagni.

situations within the time frame of his historic character. We felt very privileged when later we returned and he, after a little coaxing, broke character and talked with us interpreter to reenactor.

✑ REENACTING

Reenacting is the portrayal of events, situations or battles of our heritage.

The reenacting portion of living history has been growing immensely in popularity worldwide. It has found its niche in today's never-ending list of hobbies. There is no way to fairly count the number of reenactors, but globally one million reenactor enthusiasts could be speculated. One of the reasons we can only speculate is because there is such a vast array of types, periods and ethnic heritages being reenacted. Individuals and groups are portraying everything from the first peoples on earth to the Vietnam War, and people are champing at the bit to latch onto new time periods. The sheer volume and wide range of reenactment groups, units and blanket organizations is astounding. One only needs to search the Internet for "reenactor" to come up with over 8000 web page matches.

✑ MILITARY REENACTMENTS

One of the primary focuses of reenacting has concentrated around military living history presentations. The word "reenactment" has grown to be almost synonymous with "battle." Vast numbers of reenactors annually make pilgrimages to historic sites and battlegrounds to simulate important battles. These living historians travel in formal military units run by officers and NCOs. They boast battle honors, regulate themselves by military standards, erect period encampments and enjoy a form of true camaraderie seldom found in other hobbies.

King Louis' troops fire on a British force during the Saturday battle at a spirited encampment of Seven Years' War reenactors hosted by Fort Meigs in Perrysburg, OH. Photo by Ron Casto.

British forces return an excellent volley! We set up a very regimented military camp and structured our command "by the book" for this exciting weekend. Photo by Ron Casto.

Although many reenactment units specialize in civilian interpretation, the majority of them really enjoy the personal gratification of military interpreting. They get a kick, a true charge or adrenaline rush, from being in battle! Military units account for the largest number of amateur living history groups, and these groups often tend to be quite family oriented.

◆◆◆

BRENT: One of the most memorable experiences I've ever had in battle was about ten years ago at Old Fort Niagara in Youngstown, New York. I was portraying a sergeant of Rogers' Rangers, the famous woods-fighters of the French and Indian War era. I was given a unit of about twenty Rangers to advance down the ravelin. We leaped down from the berm and formed into two ranks that stretched from one wall of the ravelin to the other, and then we advanced slowly. From our rear a runner delivered a message that a French unit had just entered the ravelin from the opposite direction. I immediately charged my men forward. It was very realistic as both British and French volleys were erupting over us from the banks above. When we were fifty feet from the lunette (a V-shaped defensive structure pointing outward from the fort) I halted my men and reformed. Believing that the French unit in the ravelin would be charging toward us in a counter maneuver I presented my unit ready to fire. Lo and behold, around the lunette came the French unit on a dead run, straight into the sights of our muskets. I yelled, "Fire!" and with no other choice, the first ten men of the French unit crumbled, including their officer and colors, sending the remainder into a rout. We had saved our army from the French sally party, and we felt the adrenaline rush of taking part in a battle.

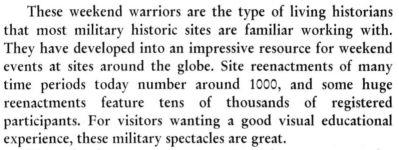

These weekend warriors are the type of living historians that most military historic sites are familiar working with. They have developed into an impressive resource for weekend events at sites around the globe. Site reenactments of many time periods today number around 1000, and some huge reenactments feature tens of thousands of registered participants. For visitors wanting a good visual educational experience, these military spectacles are great.

These battle reenactments generate large revenues for many sites and the surrounding communities. Not only do they draw huge numbers of visitors to the site's ticket booths and gift stores, but also the reenactors themselves spend their hard-earned vacation dollars there as well.

✍ EXPERIMENTAL ARCHAEOLOGY

*History is up to your interpretation
and because of this, you, the historian must strive
to utilize all avenues to find its truth.*

This form of living history is the most personal, and possibly the most gratifying. The primary focus of this art is to use reproduction clothing and gear to field test your hypotheses under similar circumstances and locations as your historic counterparts did—literally walking in their shoes. While it is sometimes difficult to include the public in this type of living history, you can develop a better historic portrayal by living as your character lived and finding out how you react to various circumstances.

When you are preparing for an historical experiment of this type, start by gathering research materials on your clothing, gear and unit (if applicable), and then look into creating similar circumstances, climate and conditions of your historic counterparts that you want to test. Your preparation is the most important aspect of your work. Lay out all your gear and clothing and ask yourself honestly, is this what they had? Would they have had this? Is this what they ate? What if? Don't ever assume, "If they'd had it, they'd have used it!"

The degree of authenticity that you want to achieve on these experiments is up to you or the group you are participating with. Decide ahead of time what you will tolerate and try your best to stick to it (i.e., food, footgear, shelter, transportation).

Our unit, Colonel Jonathan Bagley's 3rd Massachusetts Regiment, Company C, participates in several events that can be classified as experimental archaeology. One of these is our winter garrison at Colonial Michilimackinac in Mackinaw City, Michigan. We portray the guard of the garrison of this fort during the early 1760's. The main focus of this four-day event is to test your clothing and gear against the rigors of subzero weather (once it was 60 below F. with wind chill) while staying in the period guardhouse and using only the fireplace for heat. We also use period bedding of straw or feather ticks and wool blankets. One of the pleasures of the four days is to go up on the parapets and stand guard duty in the treacherous weather. Many members additionally eat period foods for the four days, but it is understood that this is not mandatory for the event. This event has given us good experiences to tell the public about when we are describing winter garrison life. It is also very enjoyable because the fort invites area school children to visit with the people in our unit and with the fort's living history staff.

These men are not Eskimos, they are members of Col. Bagley's Regiment braving the rigors of a northern Michigan winter during their experimental archaeology test at Colonial Michilimackinac, Mackinaw City, MI. (left to right, back row: Charles Tomes, Brent Kemmer II, Jeff Cunningham, John Church, Marv Davis, Mike Hartzler. Front, kneeling: Mika Hall, Matt Calder. Photo by Karen Kemmer.

BRENT: The first time I practiced experimental archaeology was many years ago. I'll never forget the experience. A friend and I were doing 1820-1830 Fur Trade era. We decided to go out and live off the land like a couple of real fur traders. We walked in with just the clothing on our backs. Each of us also had a rifle, powder horn, ball, canteen, haversack, small pack (the size of a haversack), two blankets, and we shared a tarp for a shelter. We packed in five miles and camped for five days. We took only salt, sugar and tea, and nothing else to eat! Finally, on the fourth day, late in the afternoon, we shot something: a porcupine. We carefully skinned it from the belly and decided to roast it on a stick over a fire. It really tasted great, like sweet ham, except we chewed and chewed and chewed, not knowing about the gristly glands that we should have cut off the legs (or was it that we were starving from not eating for four days?).

Here a much YOUNGER reenactor (Brent) holds the prize catch, the porcupine that allowed our fine feast! Photo by Bill Ochepick.

As we were sitting on the ground in front of our fire, eating away, all of a sudden a bow hunter walked into our camp. What a sight we must have made! We looked up; he froze, stared at us, did an abrupt about-face and took off without saying a word. We've always wondered if that guy ever got his wits back!

2

Research,
The True Starting Point

—٨٢٨٤٥٩٠٠—

Diligence is the key to research, and
research is the key to all meaningful living history.

The starting point for this hobby is *research*. This does not mean that one need spend every waking moment in an archive, but rather, the depth and intensity of his research is reflected in the depth and authenticity of his interpretation. One can utilize several types of research for living history.

First, select a time period that stimulates your intellect. Check out books, watch historical movies, and visit living history encampments, fairs and gatherings. See where your true interest lies. Once this preliminary work is done, you are ready to begin your research. And we truly recommend you do some research before jumping into living history with both feet. Just keep in mind: to be accomplished at living history you will have a never-ending need for continual research. Here we will examine the different ways you can do research.

✐ FIELD RESEARCH

Field research is the visitation to and participation in historical encampments, trade shows, historical talks or seminars, active archaeological sites and actual historical sites (both ruined and reconstructed). Some of the most valuable "research materials" at these sites are your fellow living historians. You can learn a lot by talking to them and observing their skills.

If you want to do some field research but need to find out where and when living history events are going to take place, look in the *Smoke & Fire News*. This multi-era living history newspaper not only has a full listing of era encampments, but also lists trade fairs, lectures, workshops and seminars, classifieds, parks and museums, and historical articles relating to different time periods. Longtime living historians, professionals, historic sites and novices all depend on it when they plan their own calendars. Another good source for information about upcoming events is the Internet. (See the appendices for information about *Smoke and Fire News* and reenactor web sites.)

Field research is easily accomplished but should not be the final step for those who wish to achieve perfection in their living history. These individuals and groups should venture into experimental archaeology.

✍ MOVIES & TELEVISION

When living historians utilize movies and TV for research they should beware of biases implanted by moviemakers. This is not to say that movies and TV are not a valid form of starting research, and above all a true inspiration to many living historians, especially in the off season. Many of Hollywood's versions of history are often sterile, void in historic detail, liberally derived from true historic documentation, heavily stereotyped or are fabricated solely for entertainment. This is not all bad; it is their business to entertain. As Michael Mann said often during the making of *The Last of the Mohicans*, "It's a movie, not a documentary."

BRENT: Using the movie *The Last of the Mohicans* as an example, while on the set I took notice of the facings of men portraying the 35th Regiment of Foot. They were the incorrect color but we were told they looked better on film. Also, the manual exercise was a mixture of colonial and modern, but was fabricated to accentuate the film. Finally, if looking for the true historic account of the fall of Fort William Henry, one should not use the movie or James Fenimore Cooper's book, but rather read the many primary sources or a well documented work like Ian Steele's *Betrayals*.

With TV sometimes you can obtain more accuracy from A&E and History Channel presentations. Often they are well researched and many have really started to strive for a truer portrayal of history. One director/producer who has been carving his place in this type of documentary is Gary Foreman. Mr. Foreman has a skill beyond others at utilizing living historians as extras and actors in his presentations.

✨ TRADITIONAL RESEARCH

Traditional research will take much more time. Basically, it means reading and learning as much as you can about the history, customs, clothing, food, buildings, religion, occupations, politics, leaders, wars, economy, technology, etc., of your chosen era. This is one big reason why you must narrow your time period (i.e., Greek, Roman, Viking, English Civil War, Seven Years' War, American Revolution, Napoleonic Wars, American Civil War, Spanish American War, WWI, WWII, Korean War, Vietnam, Desert Storm). Once your selection is made we recommend you read a general all-encompassing history of that period. For instance, being most familiar with the Seven Years' War, we would recommend Francis Parkman's *Montcalm and Wolfe* and Fred Anderson's *Crucible of War*.

✖ PRIMARY & SECONDARY SOURCES

Now it's time to start studying everything you can get your hands on. There are two types of information for you to study: primary and secondary sources. Primary sources are those written by the original historic peoples you are studying (i.e., letters, diaries, journals, orderly books, newspapers, family records, church records, military records). Secondary sources are books, articles and items written by authors who used primary and other secondary sources as the basis for their writing. A secondary source is an *interpretation* of other historical material.

✖ LIBRARIES

Public libraries are your best starting point. The folks who work there can be the livelihood of your research, so foster their friendship. Most librarians jump at the chance to help the truly serious researcher.

We live in a small northern Michigan community; consequently, most of the books we have wanted over the years have not been available at our local library. Fortunately our librarians are willing to help, and are excellent at acquiring many of the books and primary sources we need. The utilization of interlibrary loaning has been a savior to us in our research. Our librarians have even called archives and arranged appointments for us to visit and read primary sources that cannot be photocopied. So, develop good working relationships with your librarians.

After you have exhausted your local public library, start visiting your local college library, then your closest university library and your state library. Don't be intimidated; these libraries are just like your local facility, but larger.

❧ STARTING YOUR OWN BOOK COLLECTION

By this time you have probably come to the point in your research where you are so enthused that you have to or want to start your own personal library. Great! You're becoming a true researcher now. Many living historians have their own libraries tailored to their specific interests. Our own library, for example, contains more than three hundred books on military history of the French and Indian War and Massachusetts colonial history. We also have an extensive collection of copies of primary materials dealing with Massachusetts soldiers of the French and Indian War.

There are many ways for you to acquire books and documents for your personal library. You have undoubtedly been to living history events by now and have noticed the many sutlers or merchants who set up their tents with the living historians. Many of them have a good array of books that probably pertain to your interests.

Another good source of books are the gift and bookshops at historic sites. Two excellent examples of this can be found at Fort Ticonderoga and Old Fort Niagara in New York. These stores offer some of the finest selections of books for sale dealing with the Seven Years' War and the American Revolution. You can also order books by mail from many historic sites, book dealers and mail order companies as well as online book dealers.

❧ ARCHIVAL RESEARCH

Now you are ready to enter the most elite halls of research, your public and private archives. Some of you have been to archives and know what I mean, but many living historians have not had the privilege yet. *Archives* are repositories for rare books and primary sources. There are many archives and you will have to do a little research just to find the ones that house the information that interests you. An excellent online resource is the National Union Catalog of Manuscript Collections. The NUCMC is operated by the Library of Congress and is a gigantic bibliographic network of the holdings in hundreds of research libraries, archives, historical societies and museums.

There are a few rules of etiquette that you should be aware of before you contact or visit an archive. First, call ahead and make an appointment to visit. This often needs to be done a month or more in advance. Introduce yourself and explain what you will be looking for and the purpose of your visit. If you are aware of particular documents they house that you are interested in looking at, let them know. Many archives and libraries have online card catalogs, so you can see what is available and plan which documents to request before you even leave home.

Now that you've made your appointment and have arrived at the archive, here are some pointers. Always be on time; they are professionals and they expect you to be. Come prepared with several pencils and paper (most won't allow pens) or a laptop computer. Most archives will not let you enter the main reading rooms with coats, briefcases or bags. They will have lockers for you to leave these items in. Plan on spending all day or several days reading, for you can't take things out and they often can't make photocopies for you.

Let the archivist know what you are researching and what items you want to see. If he happens to be knowledgeable about your area of interest, he might even recommend other documents or collections relevant to your research. Then, as in any library, use the card catalog and computer database to look for references that fit your research topics, and ask to look at those items.

Now for the simple part: just sit back and read, read, read. Be sure to make scrupulous notes if you can't get copies. And above all, don't forget to write down where you get the information. As a matter of fact, write this down *first!* You'll need author, date, any collection found in, what publication, what book, copyright, pages, publisher, editor, anything, because when you get home 1000 miles away you'll not be able to go look it up again! An easy way to keep track of this information is to make a form, or use the one in Appendix 3 of this book. Make several copies of the form, and use a separate one for each source. This will be a Godsend if you ever need to look something up again, or if you plan to publish an article or a book.

❖❖❖

BRENT: About five years ago Karen, Brent II, one of his buddies and I went out to Massachusetts to do some research. My public librarian had gone the extra mile for me and had called out to the American Antiquarian Society in Worcester, Massachusetts, and made an appointment for me to do some research. The Antiquarian Society holds the orderly book of Colonel Jonathan Bagley, whose regiment we portray.

When we arrived we were very impressed, and a little intimidated. We checked in waited in a room for the archivist who was to meet me. He took us into another room and we discussed what I wanted to work on. Then he kindly called a cab for Karen and the boys and recommended a local museum for them to visit while I researched. I went into the reading room, which was a several-story, domed, open room lined with books, documents, and art. It was fabulous. I engrossed myself all day and was very satisfied when they allowed me to take a video of the orderly book. They also made a photocopy of the orderly book for my records, so I could transcribe it for my book, *Freemen, Freeholders and Citizen Soldiers*.

Near closing time, Karen and the boys came back to pick me up. I asked the archivist if it was possible to allow my wife and son to look at the orderly book. He graciously said yes and escorted them in. This was a wonderful experience for a twelve-year-old boy. He got to sit at the table and actually read and touch (with white cotton gloves of course) a 236-year-old document. We'll never forget that experience.

One last thing about research we'd like to add: Don't keep all your findings to yourself, *share them!* Too many people do all this work and never allow anyone else to see it; consequently, no one else can benefit. Keep in mind, the main reason we do living history is to *educate,* and what better way to do this than sharing or publishing your research.

3

Remember, It Takes Time & Money!

—*✻*—

Like any hobby,
reenacting can cost you a lot of time and money.

KAREN: When we first got into this hobby as a family, our
son was young and we had little money. I worked forty hours
a week as a bank teller and Brent attended college full-time
(18-21 credits a semester) and worked twenty hours a week at
the museum. We drove a 1979 Pontiac Firebird, and at events,
all three of us slept in a small wedge tent. We made all our
own clothing and gear, except the tent. We always found the
time and money to enjoy our hobby, and we are sure you can,
too.

Here are some examples of what to expect.

✐ CLOTHING

Unless you have an endless supply of money and can have
everything made for you, you're going to spend a lot of time
sewing. We made all of our clothing for about the first twelve
years. So plan "time" for that.

Back in the old days when we were just starting out in our living history venture, we used to portray Frenchmen (I hate to admit this) and Karen made all our period clothing. Here is one of our early attempts at portraying a French fur trader (Brent), his LOVELY Ojibwa wife (Karen) and their mètis (mixed blood) son (Brent II).

ॐ TIME TRAVELING

Another thing that takes up time is traveling. You probably will be traveling several hours to these events. We average 300 miles a weekend going to our living history encampments. So you'll have to think about taking time for packing meals for the road or stopping at fast food restaurants, and for making rest stops.

ॐ FOOD

Don't forget the time it takes to plan ahead for your weekend meals. We sometimes cook ahead and pack up all the food in watertight containers that go in a cooler. If you are single and are going to take only "historically correct" foods, then you won't have to worry about packing your cooler, but you will need more time to prepare your food because you won't easily be able to purchase it. You also should pack your non-perishable foods in hard containers so everything doesn't get smashed in your tent.

ॐ PACKING UP

Then there is the wonderful job of packing your vehicle. Brent usually does this the day before we leave. Hopefully you can fit everything in, and yes, that includes room for your husband and kids! Plan on this task taking from thirty minutes to two hours, depending on if it's for just one person or for a family that takes too much stuff.

And don't forget, everything you pack has to be unpacked and set up when you arrive! Plan on another thirty minutes to two hours. Oops—forgot to mention—You'll have to pack it all up again at the end of your event, and then when you get home you'll have to unpack it one last time. But don't let all this packing and unpacking scare you.

Oh, did you think you were done once you got back home? Not yet!

Some other chores that take time will happen after you arrive home and you've unpacked. You will have to mend things, wash clothing, wash dishes and clean out your food containers and cooler. Then after all this is done you will have to put it all away and store it for next time. And don't forget, everyone will want to get into the shower and scrub off 48 hours' worth of dirt! Many of our friends also spend hours every week reading and researching.

Don't worry, after, say about twenty years, you'll get it down to a science, until you decide to change your portrayal or you want to get more stuff!

✐ MONEY MATTERS

Obviously, all this will cost money, but you've got to expect that. No hobby is cheap! Depending on the time period you choose to portray, and how in-depth you go, you can start out with a minimal investment of $200 to $2000! Keep in mind, $200 isn't going to get you very much unless you make it all very cheaply! This is only for one person as well; don't forget the clothing and gear for your spouse and kids if you're coming on board as a family!

Add in the travel costs such as gasoline, wear and tear on your vehicle, equipment such as a car-top carrier for your stuff, motels or campground fees, and meals on the road. Don't forget to allow yourself some spending money for books for your research library, or that special item you just have to buy from the sutler!

Fear not! There are also some ways you can save money. Some military units have extra clothing and gear to lend to get people started, but these aren't always the best items and you will be expected to get your own stuff as soon as possible. If a unit offers this to you, we recommend taking advantage of it to make sure you like doing reenacting and that you fit in with that unit before you put out the big bucks. Our unit has items to lend beginners, but we urge them to get their own clothing and equipment as quickly as possible.

One cost factor to keep in mind with reenacting is that it may be fully or partially tax-deductible for you. Now don't quote us on this, we're not tax professionals. Many reenacting units have a non-profit, tax-exempt, educational status. Most national and state organizations have this status as well. Many individuals and groups can join these units. Some of the historic sites that you do demonstrations for have this status too. From what we understand, and what our tax man tells us, if you or your unit belongs to one of these tax-exempt organizations or participates in educational programs at these sites, you can claim "non-cash, charitable deductions" on your federal taxes. Of course you must be able to use the long form for this deduction, but it's worth asking your taxman about.

After all, if you're spending a lot of money giving educational demonstrations and talks all over the place, why not take advantage of this deduction if it is applicable for you? According to the IRS, a charitable donation is money or property donated to a qualified charitable organization. Such donations are deductible on Schedule A as an itemized deduction on your federal taxes.

—◆◆—

When we came to a point in our lives where we both decided to change careers, we actively chose teaching, partially because it fits so naturally with our love of educational living history. Our time seems twice as well spent, because our careers feed our hobby and our hobby feeds our careers!

So be organized, plan ahead and get packing!

"Turn over the wagon and form a circle, men, here they come!" You can't beat the aesthetics of an historic site for reenacting. Colonial Michilimackinac in Mackinaw City, Michigan, for example, hosts many annual events for colonial reenactors during its public season. Here Col. Bagley's regiment takes aim in one of the fort's summer programs. (Left to right: Dan Kortes, Marv Davis, John Calder [standing], Matt Calder, Tim Anderson, Andy Davis, Jeff Cunningham, Brent Kemmer II.) Photo by Karen Kemmer.

During this colors ceremony at Green's Village Greenville, Michigan, you can see some of the diversity of reenacted time periods from 1754-1945. Photo by Brent Kemmer.

Some reenactors really get carried away in our hobby! What lucky one of you owns his own Sherman Tank (and Karen complained when I got my cannon!)? Photo by Brent Kemmer.

Don't let her size fool you! "Dorothy," our light 3-pounder, packs the wallop of a heavy gun! Another toy for the boys...I mean reenactors. (Left to right: Andy Davis, Brent Kemmer II [cannon maker], Marv Davis, author Brent Kemmer, John Timberlake, Paul Timberlake, Matt Calder.) Photo by Karen Kemmer.

❧ 4 ❧

You'll Need A Few Things

—ᴧᴧᴧ✳ᴧᴧᴧ—

Reenactors are the world's greatest packrats.
We constantly need more stuff, good stuff.

Now that you have started to organize your moneys for your
hobby it's time to take an in-depth look at a breakdown of it
all. Making general statements about reenacting is difficult
because of the differences in time periods and the varying
degrees of technology throughout history. But, here's a go at
it.

There are many items that you can attempt to make if
you're trying to save money or if you just enjoy crafting your
own things. Some of you will find it easy to make your
clothing and some of you will find it easier to make your gear.
Some of you might discover that attempting to make any of it
is a disaster and a waste of time.

How do you make a Desert Storm era grenade, or a WWI
gas mask, or a Roman Centurion breastplate, or a Thompson
Machine Gun, or a Korean War helmet, or a real powdered
hair wig for an officer of the American Revolution? There are
many items that you just won't be able to make unless you
have special talents. We have several machinists in our unit,
and they come up with some neat items, but there is no way
the rest of us can even begin to understand how to make
them.

ᘒᨪᨦ SUTLERS

You might need to rely on the professionals, your period sutlers and merchants, for the items that you don't want to make or can't make. Those of us who reenact the French and Indian War era depend on the many good sutlers who not only follow our military units to encampments, but many of them also operate mail-order businesses and retail stores. (See Appendix 5.)

There are also several fine period seamstresses and tailors available for us. Once you've become active in your chosen historical period, other living historians can put you in touch with your period outfitters as well.

Now let's break things down into categories.

ᘒᨪᨦ TENTS

*The dwellings and abodes of the past
become excellent educational tools for the present.*

A tent is one of those pieces of equipment that 99.9% of you won't even think of trying to make and we don't recommend it. There are excellent period tent smiths out there who make great quality tents for all periods. (See Appendix 5.) If you're doing living history of recent eras, you can shop at your local "army surplus."

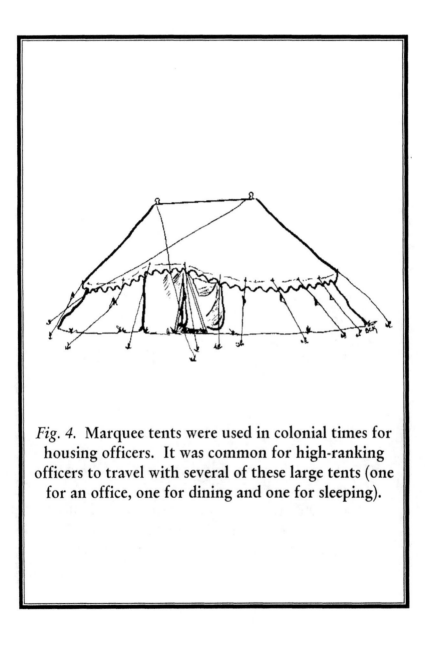

Fig. 4. Marquee tents were used in colonial times for housing officers. It was common for high-ranking officers to travel with several of these large tents (one for an office, one for dining and one for sleeping).

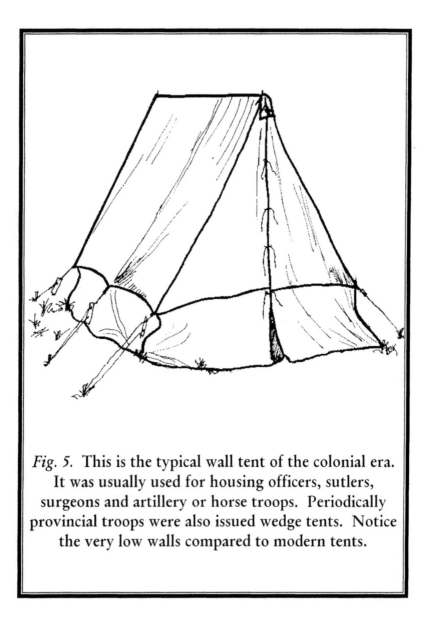

Fig. 5. This is the typical wall tent of the colonial era. It was usually used for housing officers, sutlers, surgeons and artillery or horse troops. Periodically provincial troops were also issued wedge tents. Notice the very low walls compared to modern tents.

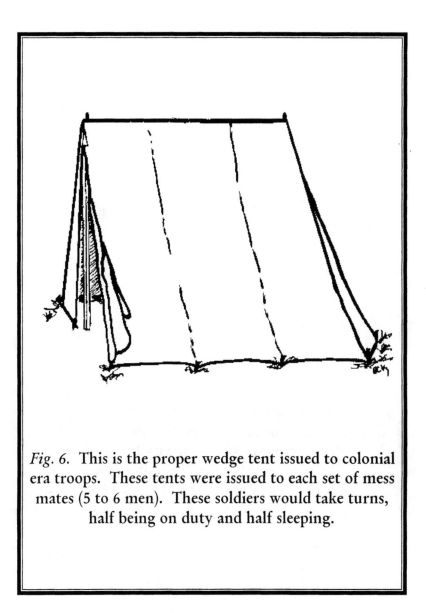

Fig. 6. This is the proper wedge tent issued to colonial era troops. These tents were issued to each set of mess mates (5 to 6 men). These soldiers would take turns, half being on duty and half sleeping.

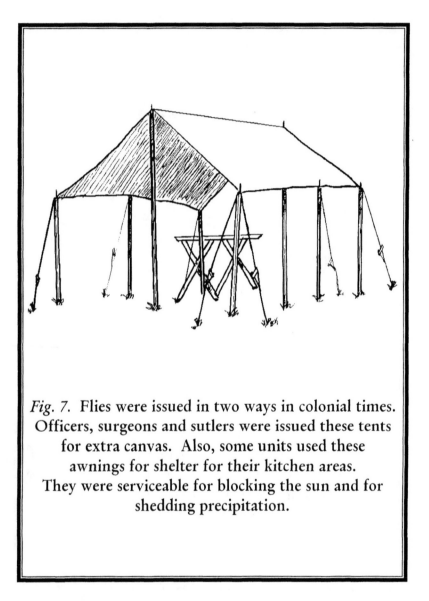

Fig. 7. Flies were issued in two ways in colonial times. Officers, surgeons and sutlers were issued these tents for extra canvas. Also, some units used these awnings for shelter for their kitchen areas. They were serviceable for blocking the sun and for shedding precipitation.

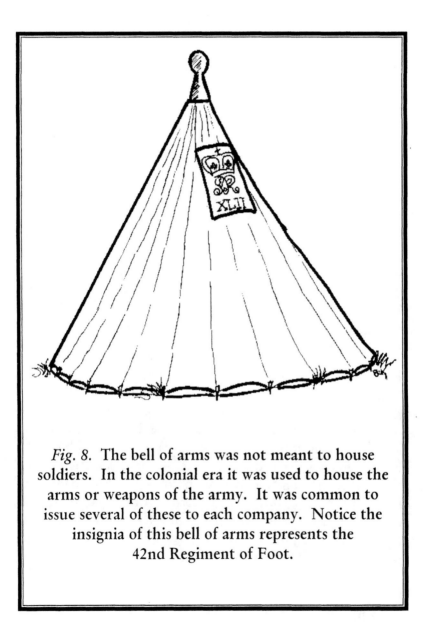

Fig. 8. The bell of arms was not meant to house soldiers. In the colonial era it was used to house the arms or weapons of the army. It was common to issue several of these to each company. Notice the insignia of this bell of arms represents the 42nd Regiment of Foot.

Tents will be one of the most expensive items for you as a military reenactor. Plan on spending $100 on up to $1000. Pup tents and shelter halves can be very reasonable compared to colonial tents, which range from $165 to $500. We recommend that you get all the "bells and whistles" when ordering your tent. For instance, if ordering a colonial wedge tent, get a ground cloth made for your tent and order your tent with sod cloths and overlapping door flaps. Also, make sure you order mildew resistant and flame retardant canvas. (It pays off. We have a tent that's 10 years old, and one that we sold to another reenactor that is now 15 years old and still being used).

Make sure that you thoroughly research the type of tent appropriate for your era and portrayal, and find out exactly what your unit requires. For example, if you're portraying a British regular private soldier you sure aren't going to have a marquee, wall tent or large wedge tent! You should have a wedge tent ranging from 6x6 to 8x8. Do your research, save your money!

◆◆◆

KAREN: When we started out, we couldn't afford *squat*. So a friend and Brent decided to make our tent. We were portraying French militia, so they draped a piece of canvas over three sticks tied into a tripod and staked it to the ground, leaving it open in front. That was OK for Brent and his buddy Bill. Then they decided they wanted to have something more substantial, hoping to entice his friend's wife, our babies and me into camping with them instead of in a separate modern camp. (Yes, that's correct! For the first few years I would stay in a modern camp with Brent II while Brent stayed in his period camp with the other fellows.)

Brent and Bill then took their canvas tarp and draped it over poles simulating a *very* crude wedge tent. Unfortunately it didn't have a front or back, so there was no way I was staying in it! Then they got the idea of sewing blankets to the front and back—Whoopee! Finally, they got more canvas and sewed on a proper back and front flaps. I still don't know how all six of us could have stayed in it. It was only 4x6 wide and 3 feet tall. Brent and Bill used it for about another year, even though they never made it waterproof. Then somehow we scraped together enough money and BOUGHT our first tent, a 10x10x7 "wedge" tent. This was our home away from home for several years.

Once we finished earning our teaching degrees, all hell broke loose! We purchased a 6x9 bell-back wedge, then a 10x12 marquee, then an 8x8 marquee, then a 10x12 fly (awning), then we sold the 10x12 marquee, then we bought a 10x12 wall tent, then we sold the 8x8 marquee, then we made a bell of arms, then bought an 8x8 wedge, then a 12x15 mess fly, then bought back the 8x8 marquee (no Winnebago yet) and NOW we still have the 6x9 wedge, 8x8 wedge, 8x8 marquee, both flies, the bell of arms, and of course we still have remnants of the original little makeshift wedge tent that we rip pieces off and make things out of once in a while. Of all these, we only really use the two wedge tents, 8x8 marquee and the smaller fly any more. (Maybe it's time to sell canvas again!)

🐜 🐜 🐜 🐜 🐜 🐜 🐜 🐜 🐜 🐜 🐜

(Not *that* kind of fly!)

ᶜ⁄ᵒ EQUIPMENT

Equipment can be the savior or burden of an army.

The term "equipment" refers to everything from personal belongings to camp furniture. Always keep in mind that what you carry and set up needs to reflect your portrayal, your personal standing in your time period (i.e., farmer, private soldier, officer, landed gentry, slave), and, if you are military, your rank. Consequently, whether your portrayal is civilian or military you should be able to explain how you got your equipment there. If you portray a civilian you may have brought it with you on a converted hippie bus (1969). If you're portraying a WWII private, you carried it on your back. If you were an 18th century soldier, you and the rest of your company brought it in a bateau or wagon. If you're a slave it was rolled up in your blanket. If you're a Napoleonic officer, it was carried by your servant and on a cart pulled by a team of horses.

For example, if you are portraying a British soldier in the French and Indian War, here is a list of your equipment:

firelock
sling
hammer cap
stopper
waist belt
hanger
sword knot
scabbard
bayonet and scabbard
tomahawk and cover
cartridge pouch with belt
buckles
rounds
brush
wire
worm

turnkey
oil bottle
rag
flints and steel
knapsack with strap & buckles
clothes brush
pair shoe brushes
black ball
handkerchief
combs
knife and spoon
haversack
blanket
strap and garters
canteen with string & stopper.

Every five to six men were also issued several items to share: a tent with ropes, poles and pins, a camp kettle with bag, and a camp axe. If you have much more than this you truly can't be doing a proper portrayal. Once again, be sure to do your research. Many colonial military reenactors carry cast-iron cook gear; this is incorrect for that period. There is no documentation of cast-iron cooking gear being issued, but there are a lot of listings of tin and a few brass ten-quart camp kettles. There are also some listings of platters, bowls and "flesh brushes" for some units.

Bed sacks, tickings, sheets, pillows and lanterns were issued in barracks. If you have made a commitment to yourself, or if you are in a unit of "hard-cores," this is all you should have. Most units, though, are not going to stop you from being more comfortable, if you do it discreetly. For instance, in our unit we allow people to have a chair and a trunk as well. Inside their tent they can have a cot or sleep on the ground. (We don't force 5 to 6 guys to share one tent.)

We try to limit the number of flies (awnings) in our camp so that they are only used as mess flies. (We'll talk about camp set-ups in Chapter 10). We do make a conscience effort to ask our members to limit their camp furniture. If items need to be hidden, we conceal them under our cots or put them in authentic-looking boxes, barrels or bags.

The main idea though, at least to our way of thinking, is that this is a family oriented hobby for the most part, and some exceptions must be made on their behalf. Secondly, a man should be able to have a chair, stool, bench or box to sit on in the shade after coming out of battle on an 80 to 90 degree, humid summer day! But if you belong to a unit that believes in total limitation, then have at it! You're committed 100%, and should be commended!

✐ SAFETY

There are also several "modern" items that we recommend taking with you. At the very least, each unit should have a first aid kit. If you're going it alone, you should have your own kit. This should not be overlooked. Sooner or later you or a member in your unit will need it and basic first aid could possibly even save a life.

Another consideration is fire pit protection. This can assume several different forms. We recommend every fire have at least one period fire bucket. It is also a good idea to have a fire extinguisher in every unit's camp. This can be in a designated tent or outside with a period-looking cover over it. Just make sure everyone knows where it is and how to use it.

✑ MODERN NECESSITIES

The one piece of equipment that the majority of you are going to have to bring is a cooler. Even though it's a proper portrayal to have the bloody flux, most of us really don't wish to reenact this. There are several ingenious ways that have been used to disguise coolers. My sergeant uses a box lined with foam isolation for his cooler making it look like a supply box. One of my soldiers uses a fitted canvas cover, which gives his cooler the appearance of a military parcel. (With military markings it's quite believable.) The simplest thing to do is to drape a period blanket or a piece of canvas over it. You could also just keep it in your tent, but we recommend you set up the inside of your tent for interpreting as well—the public loves to peer inside an open tent.

One modern item that is worth its weight in gold at camp is a box of moistened baby wipes, concealed in an appropriate container, of course.

BRENT: One final note on equipment is to make sure you keep it in good repair. You'll find out quickly that you'll grow to depend on the few comforts that you allow yourself. A group of us learned this lesson the hard way about twelve years ago.

We were sitting around the campfire when Karen leaned back on her stool and, Crash! The stool broke, she hit the ground, her dress flew up and she slowly rose to her feet. Being a gallant gentleman, one of our friends went to his camp and retrieved another stool for her.

She gently eased herself down and, Crash! She broke the second stool into splinters. This time as she rose, she picked the stool up and pitched it into the fire, with a few choice words.

Later that evening she reverted to sitting in a chair. Everything was fine until the back legs of the chair sank into the soft sod and she toppled over in total embarrassment. Being a caring group of reenactors, at the next event they bestowed upon her a document signed by the King and proclaiming her his official furniture tester!

Karen Kemmer,
I do proclaim you
Royal Tester of Furniture!

✌ CLOTHING

Suave, dapper, and debonair; filthy, soiled, and vagabond;
if you portray it you'd better dress the part.

You may decide to make your own period clothing or to buy it. You can make many of the items you'll need, depending on your skill level as a seamstress or tailor. Patterns and fabrics are available for civilian clothing from almost any era. Women's outfits of most eras can be reproduced. If you need military clothing, you can probably make most things yourself if it is pre-1860's, but around the time of the American Civil War, both military and civilian men's clothing designs became more tailored and complicated. It's best to have these garments made by professional costume makers who specialize in clothing for living historians. If you've been around for a while and money isn't as big a deal as it once was, by all means have the professionals make all your historical clothing.

BRENT: When we started out in living history, Karen made all of our historical clothing. Then she got fed up and told me "If you want another uniform, you can make it yourself!" So I had her show me how to use the sewing machine, and I've made my own uniforms for quite a few years now. I find the uniform coats and waistcoats to be quite easy to make, but I am contemplating having my next one made professionally. The last few years we have really slacked off on making our own outfits and prefer having custom period clothing made for us. We have to admit it's quite a luxury, and it's a relief not to have to toil over the machine.

For all eras there are clothing articles that you're not going to be able to make. Shoes and boots, for instance, are going to be impossible unless you're a cobbler, and if you are you might as well make them for everyone else and pay for your hobby! Socks and hose can be made but I've only heard of two or three reenactors who have made them. Hats beyond the colonial period are impossible for most of us to fabricate. With the superb quality of goods made by the seamstresses and tailors who work for themselves and for the period sutlers and merchants, we recommend that you have them make most of your clothing if you can afford it. Just make sure you look for authenticity in your selections through personal research, and check to see if your unit has minimum requirements that you must meet.

Our unit has drafted the following list of the minimum required clothing for soldiers to be able to participate with us at living history events:

* Shirt (colonial design / 1740's-1763)
* Neck covering (colonial design / 1740's-1763)
* Breeches (colonial design / 1740's-1763)
* Stockings (colonial design / 1740's-1763)
* Shoes (colonial design shoes, boots, moccasins / 1740's-1763)
* Waistcoat (colonial design / 1740's-1763)*
* Hat (colonial design / 1740's-1763, tricorn preferred)
* [A work or hunting shirt could temporarily replace a waistcoat / colonial design 1740's-1763]
* Within a year a recruit should outfit himself with the proper soldier's coat and tricorn hat

Some other units have much stricter minimum requirements. For example, if you were to portray a soldier of a regular regiment of foot in the British army, you would probably be required to have a full uniform before you could take the field with the rest of the regiment, and this, in our opinion, is warranted. How can you represent British regulars if you're not in uniform?

You'll probably choose to make some of your own items, and there is a certain satisfaction in doing so. For instance, Karen finds chemises cheap and easy to make, and prefers to make her own. There are also items that you will find very difficult to make. We have found that breeches tend to be one of the most difficult items of our clothing and never even think of making them any more.

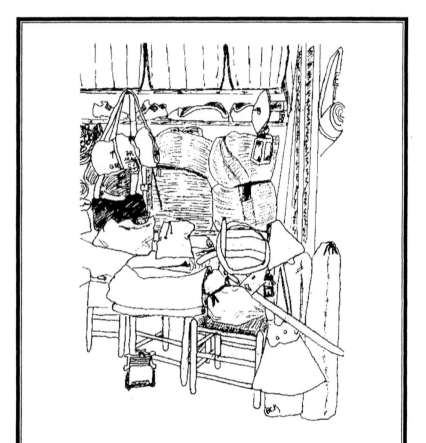

Fig. 10. This is the storage shelving in our garage. These are the items that we take with us most often. Notice we have several long shelves attached to the studs and we have placed our gear in plastic tubs on the top shelf. Blankets and smaller items are stored on the next two shelves and on our camp chairs. We generally just stack our tent poles against the wall as seen on the right.

ᢒᡐ How To Store It All

Organize, or you'll be the one
who always comes to camp saying, "I forgot..."

Now that you've got all this wonderful historical stuff, how and where are you going to store it all? The key is,

✂ GET ORGANIZED! ✂

Many of you will not be graced with having a garage for storage, so you will have to hunt to find places for your items. If you live in an apartment, you are lucky if a storage unit is included in your rent. If so, we hope you don't have anything else to store in it, because you'll really have a lot now! If you don't have a storage unit, you have two choices: you can buy a nice weather-tight storage trailer and leave your gear in it all the time, or you're going to have to learn to live with the stuff in your apartment!

Maybe you're lucky enough to have a basement, spare closet or attic. These are not the best of places to be carrying things in and out of every weekend, but you might have no other choice.

If you are lucky enough to have a garage with your house or rental home, you've got it made, *if* you can keep your garage clean. (What a novel idea, having a clean garage!) Now, if you're ready to get started, here's what we recommend you do (all these ideas hold true for basements, closets, attics or garages).

First, lay out all your clothing and equipment and take a good visual survey of what you have and how much room you think you will need to store it all.

Second, draw up a plan of storage units, plastic tubs, hanging clothes racks and/or shelving. We recommend that you store everything off the ground. This will keep things cleaner and also protect it in case of water on the floor.

Now that your plan is set on paper, go and purchase the storage items you need. Our favorite storage arrangements are open shelves and hanging clothing racks. We have one of the best setups: not only do we have a garage, which we keep clean, but we also have an enclosed, attached lean-to on our garage. So our setup is quite extensive (and we need it for all our junk—we mean, stuff). We have one storage area for things we use every weekend and a separate area for items that we rarely or never use. We also have a worktable for items that need to be repaired or otherwise prepared for the next event.

In the lean-to we have a wall of shelves for items we almost never use any more. This is also where we keep boxes of fabric and fabric scraps. We also have a clothing rack in this room and some other shelves for items that we periodically use, but may be seasonal.

We have two types of shelving. One is the inexpensive metal shelving you can pick up at discount stores and hardware stores. This is good for lighter items and for shallow shelf space. The other shelves are more substantial. We purchased metal shelf brackets that slide into metal slatted strips screwed to the studs in the garage. Then we purchased and cut 1 x 10 planks for the actual shelves. These will hold a reasonable weight and give you an ample shelf width.

We have two methods of storing hanging clothes. For the first method we simply bought some large spike nails and rubber-coated hooks that are driven or screwed into the wall studs. Another way is to rig up a makeshift closet rod. We took some nylon strapping and made two even loops of the length that we wanted the rack to hang off the ground. These were screwed securely to the roof rafters. Then we took a ½ inch piece of round aluminum stock and laid it inside the loops. (Make sure when you secure the loops to the rafters that they are not farther apart than your stock metal.) We used the aluminum because we had it lying around, but you could use cold rolled steel or just a thick wooden dowel or closet rod.

Now you're set to place your clothes and equipment on your shelving and hangers.

There are several additional suggestions regarding the organization of your storage areas. You will have items that will need repair and you will need a place to put things until everything is clean and ready to put into storage until the next time. We have an old workbench that measures 36 x 48 inches and is waist-high. It also has four drawers under the top, which are nice for tools and small supplies. The bench is on casters, making it movable. This worktop has been one of the most useful of our storage items.

Another helpful hint is to use plastic tubs. If your storage areas are anything like ours, it is possible for mice, squirrels and insects to get into your clothing and gear. We use plastic or rubber tubs and plastic garbage cans to put all our clothing and gear in during the winter, and also for items that we don't use, or hardly use any more. This may seem expensive, but if you watch out for sales you can pick up these items quite cheaply, for about $4 to $12.

Now, there is one more storage option for your clothes and gear. This is how we "store" some of the items that we don't use any more, but you could do this with objects that you use more often as well. You can decorate your house or apartment with them! Just take a look at any home decorating book that features colonial or country decor and you'll see many examples of period items being used as accessories. Also, you'll notice a great number of trunks and storage containers being used as furniture. We have taken this even further and totally decorated our home in 18th century style using some of our "stuff," and purchasing many other items specifically for decorating.

No matter how you decide to store your items, the key is to organize or you'll never find anything, and you'll always haul too much!

✒ TRANSPORTATION

*You can either do a lot of planning and organizing
or buy a much bigger vehicle and a very large trailer.*

Now that you have made or purchased your clothes and gear,
and you've got it all organized and stored nicely and neatly,
how are you going to haul all of it to the next event? This may
be where your ingenuity will really pay off. Many people don't
have full-sized pickups, vans or enclosed weatherproof trailers.
Again, your starting point is to take stock of all your clothing
and gear that you are going to take with you.

✒ THE TENT POLE CHALLENGE

One of the biggest challenges is how to transport your tent
poles. If your vehicle isn't large enough to carry them inside,
you will need to secure them to the outside. This can be done
in three ways:

  ＊ You can put something protective (a blanket or pad)
     on your vehicle roof and securely strap your poles
     down on it
  ＊ You can strap them to your roof rack, if you happen to
     have one or
  ＊ You can purchase a set of roof rack poles.

We have used all three methods in our travels over the years
and have had great success. Some reenactors even put their

poles in PVC pipes and strap them to their roof racks. Just secure them well; you don't really want to impale any cars behind you on the expressway (that type of behavior should be kept for battles).

∽ "HONEY, DID YOU REMEMBER TO PACK THE CANNON?"

Another challenge is figuring out ways to fit everything in. If you're going it alone you should have no problem with any size vehicle, as long as you have the willpower to limit your gear appropriately. When it comes to a family, though, it's much more difficult to stow all the clothing, bedding, tents, food, etc. for several people, but it can be done!

We have traveled as a family to living history events in an array of vehicles:

* 1971 Ford full sized station wagon
* 1979 Pontiac Firebird
* 1988 Ford Escort wagon
* 1991 Dodge Dynasty
* 1991 Dodge Ram truck
* 1993 Dodge Ram conversion van
* 1995 Dodge Neon
* 1998 Chevy Lumina
* 1999 GMC Sierra king cab truck

One thing that has helped us over the years was an enclosed roof top carrier. They can be purchased for about $75 on up, and are very utilitarian. These carriers will augment your vehicle's carrying capacity by doubling your trunk space. You can, as we often do, use the car top carrier and the roof racks together.

Fig. 11. Since our son has taken off for college we have weeded down our camp (for some events) to fit in our Chevrolet Lumina. Notice that we travel with a hard plastic car top carrier and strap our tent poles securely to our roof racks.

If you're lucky enough to have a truck or a van, you're in better shape, at least for ease of packing and unpacking your vehicle. We highly recommend the use of a topper or tonneau cover for your pickup bed. With our full-sized pickup and conversion van, we have been able to take all of our camp equipment, including our light three-pound cannon, and four adults with lots of room.

You also may want to purchase or already have a weather-tight trailer to pull with your truck or van. Some reenactors have some real slick travel/storage set-ups with very organized shelving inside of them.

When our son was younger we always brought along 3 or 4 of his teen-aged friends. We traveled in our full sized van, but with six people inside we needed more room for our gear, so I purchased a 4x10-foot trailer and refurbished it, making it weather-tight. We carried enough stuff for an entire company of soldiers! When we pulled up, people thought the circus had arrived. We would set up our 10x12 marquee, 8x8 marquee, 10x12 fly, 8x8 wedge, 6x9 wedge and bell of arms. We also carried a mess fly for our unit, a drum, camp pennants to mark out our camp, stakes and roping to rope off our unit's camp, and all the clothing and personal gear for six! We even took a bookshelf, desk and six chairs. It was a Godsend having those four teen-aged boys to help set it all up. We were a real group of OVER PACKERS! Just keep in mind, you don't have to take everything you own.

Our biggest challenge was when we were just getting started. We had our Pontiac Firebird. Any of you who have been in one knows you have front bucket seats, a small back seat and a tiny trunk. Obviously Karen and I took up the front seats and we had to strap Brent II into the back in his car seat. Luckily his legs weren't too long, because we had items on the floor piled up to his feet. Beside and behind him we had packed all our soft items, both loose and in bags. (If we ever had gotten in an accident he wouldn't have been hurt, but the paramedics probably wouldn't have seen him in there either!)

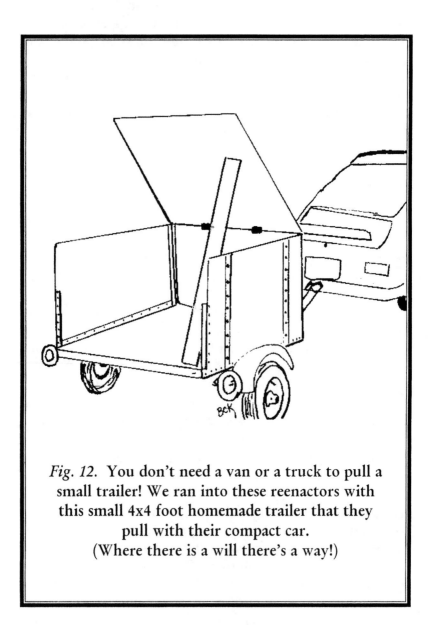

Fig. 12. You don't need a van or a truck to pull a small trailer! We ran into these reenactors with this small 4x4 foot homemade trailer that they pull with their compact car.
(Where there is a will there's a way!)

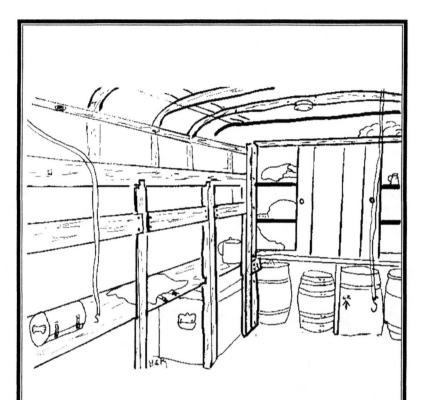

Fig. 13. This reenactor, like many who are fortunate enough to have aluminum storage trailers, has rigged the interior into a grand storage unit. Not only can you transport your equipment more safely this way, but you can store it in a trailer like this instead of inside your house, apartment or garage.

We didn't have a car top carrier yet, so we rolled our tent poles up in a blanket and tied them down to the roof by running ropes through the windows and around the roof of the car. But for our bedding and tent, we rolled all the blankets up, then rolled them up in our tent, and then rolled all of that up in our ground cloth. Then we took this giant roll and tied it onto the trunk lid and rear spoiler. It looked like a huge blanket roll on a horse! But it worked real slick and nothing got wet in our bedroll. We wouldn't recommend this arrangement, though, if you have claustrophobia.

As you see, it *can* be done. After twenty years, we now have it all planned out. If we are taking our son and/or friends and/or our cannon, we can take our pickup. If only two of us are traveling, we can just take our Lumina. One member of our unit has figured out how to consolidate his gear into a very small space, and he has made quite a spectacle of himself riding his Harley into camp!

✍ How To Turn Comfort Into Misery

You don't have to travel with everything you own unless you're portraying Caesar, Tutankhamen, George Washington, Napoleon, Pershing, or Eisenhower.

Take some advice: don't carry everything you have accumulated to camp. If you're the packrat type, don't let it follow you to your living history camp. We have a lot of stuff, enough to outfit at least 20 men and boys and 6 women, but we have really cut back. You will find as you get started that you will have the urge to get lots of stuff and you will want to take it to show it off to your new friends. That is part of getting into the hobby, but it can take you over.

You will go through periodic cleansings when you'll sort through your clothing and gear and weed out unnecessary items. If you don't need it, don't carry it to camp. We recommend that you try as hard as you can to limit your travel clothing and gear to just your personal comforts. Now, this is very abstract, and we guess it needs to be, because everyone's ideas of comfort are different. The key is to keep your amount of toting to a level that will allow you comfort, but will not burn you out as you set up and tear down your camp. After all, you're supposed to be enjoying yourself!

If we were to give you a guideline, it would be this: if it takes much more than an hour for your family to set up or tear down, you're taking too much stuff. Unless you're a high-ranking officer, an individual person should not take more than 30 to 45 minutes to set up.

We can set up and tear down easily in 45 minutes to an hour, and if it's going to rain we can do it in half an hour or less! You need to strive for a balance between Spartan and comfort, without spending all day unloading and setting up.

(Travelin' Light)

Here we are, the three of us (authors Karen and Brent Kemmer, and son Brent II) that you've been reading about in this book. This is probably how you will see us dressed if you see us at events. (Boy, I'm a handsome devil!)

✍ 5 ✍

Including Your Family

—✿—

*Given the chance, reenacting can be the number one,
favorite family hobby for you, your spouse and your kids.
There's something for everyone.*

KAREN: When we first got into reenacting, I was a bit
reluctant. It all seemed so foreign to me, "the modern-day
queen." After all, my idea of roughing it was staying at a
motel with no indoor pool! And taking a baby or toddler who
was not potty trained was simply out of the question!

✍ EASE INTO IT

The first few times that I went to events with Brent, we were
lucky enough to get relatives to watch our son. If an event
took place near a family member's home, Brent II would stay
with them, or we would visit Dad for the day at camp and
sleep in the comfort of their home at night. Actually, staying
fulltime at an event was something Brent II and I eased into,
one step at a time.

When I started going to encampments I met plenty of
friendly, helpful women who also had young children in tow.
When Brent II was about two years old (and potty trained) we
started taking him along with us, and we found there were
always other kids for him to play with. One nice thing is that

everyone pretty much watches out for everyone else's kids. It is one the safest places for young families.

Our unit, like many others, really tries hard to give kids responsibility so that they feel included in the activities. They start out carrying wood and water, and before you know it, they start carrying our flags and drum while marching with us. When they're old enough we also start teaching them safety and respect for the muskets, because they will want to fight in the battles some day.

I started attending about eight to ten events for the next ten years. At one time we got up to 27 events a year (too much)! Now we're back to about 12.

✍ WILD WOMEN?

The first full weekend I stayed at camp, I hooked up with some wives from Rogers' Rangers. We had a blast after the kids went to bed that Saturday night! To begin with, we sat around the fire and had a couple of drinks. (They gave me my Indian name that night: "Two Beers.") Someone came up with the idea of running our husbands' underwear up the flagpole to see if they would notice in the morning! After all, they were at another campfire talking about "Rob Rogers."

We women spread out and went from camp to camp collecting "clean" underwear to run up the flagpole. We were laughing so hard that the men started to get suspicious. Being good Rangers, they followed us, trying to keep under cover. When they saw us running a pair of underwear up the pole, they jumped out of the bushes and quickly took them down.

Someone yelled, "Stop those women!" but we made our getaway. From that night on we were known as the "Rangerettes," troublemakers who pulled jokes at several events.

The underwear incident has become legend now, and believe it or not, *I* have been blamed for the whole thing (untrue)! In fact, once someone took a Ranger officer's sign off his travel trailer at an event at Colonial Michilimackinac, and a year later it showed up on his barracks door at Old Fort Niagara. And would you believe, the officer thought it was I, and I think he still does to this day! It just *happened* that I came up the stairs as he noticed his sign was back. (Shhhhh! It was really an officer of the 80th Regiment of Foot who took it...Of course, you didn't hear it from *me*. Shhhhh!)

∾ LASTING FRIENDSHIPS

I found that the camp life after the public has gone can be the most fun, and friendships are easily made. Many women cook, chase kids, sew or do crafts during the day, but at night we can relax and just enjoy the company of our peers and absorb the surroundings in peace. As our son got older he played with other kids and by 9 p.m. he would tell me "I'm going to bed." Sometimes he'd want me to lie down with him and tell him a story, and I always did. The only problem was that I often fell asleep with him, but soon my friends would come looking for me.

My son has made good friends and still sees them from time to time at big events. Most have started college now or are working full time. He loves our hobby and says he will continue to reenact his whole life. (I hope so, or it will devastate his dad!) It hardly seems possible that someone who used to sneak his "Pooh bear" to camp is now our unit's corporal, as well as a college student!

Reenacting is something our family has done for many years now. True, at first I took baby steps, easing Brent II and myself into it, but I'm not sorry. Once I found friends with common interests and it was clear Brent II was happy playing with his friends, making the transition from non-reenactor to today has been easy.

I also saw my husband's love for this hobby and decided that this was a good thing that we could all share in and learn from. It also beats having a husband who hunts and fishes or watches sports on TV all the time.

So there wasn't always a pool, but we could always stick our heads in a bucket!

✍ TRAVEL, VACATION & EVENTS

Why not kill two birds with one musket ball?
Make a vacation out of your reenactments.

Sometimes you'll want to attend an event that is quite some distance away from home, so you'll need to plan to spend some extra time on the road. At most events, Fridays are set aside for camp setup. Most of our unit tries to arrive before dark and we get set up and sometimes go out to eat together. On Saturday and Sunday there are scheduled events that we take part in. Most encampments close to the public between 3 and 5 p.m. so you can pack up and prepare to drive home. This allows you to get home by dark or shortly after.

We sometimes attend events as far as 600 miles from home, though. There is no way we can travel that far in just a weekend and attempt to enjoy ourselves. What we like to do, and what we recommend you do periodically, is to make a vacation out of it. We are both trained in history and Brent II really enjoys it too, so we often visit as many historic sites, museums and archives as we can. We know this isn't the cup of tea for all of you, but it helps us in our living history and our teaching. You can often find other, non-history-related activities for a "normal" vacation, such as swimming, snow skiing, visiting relatives or just driving around to see what you can see and relax.

BRENT: One of the most enjoyable times we had was several years ago when we went to the annual encampments at Fort Ticonderoga and Old Fort Niagara. These French and Indian War events in New York are held on back-to-back weekends. This proved to be the inspiration for our unit to take a vacation together. Six families decided to go out to Ticonderoga, participate in the event, and sightsee at all the historic places between there and Niagara during the intervening week. We had been going there for many years and had visited most of the sites, so we acted as tour guides for the others. We found a great little motel in the town of Ticonderoga and stayed there from Friday through Monday. After the event was over, on Monday we took the group to the nearby sites. In the afternoon the men wanted to see a few other sites but the women wanted to shop. Karen took the ladies around town and I took the men to see where some of the other forts and battle sites were.

The next three days we slowly traveled west toward Niagara, stopping at forts and museums, and really enjoying the group's interest in history. Then near Rome, New York, we got tired of staying in motels, so we decided to rent some KOA camp cabins and have a barbeque. As we unpacked it started to rain, but we still had our barbeque, and that evening turned out to be one of the most enjoyable times we have ever spent with our members, despite the rain! Since then we have talked about taking other group vacations with our reenacting unit. We think you also might like to try this kind of vacation. It's fun, family-oriented and educational, as well as a great way to build camaraderie with your unit.

"Really, Dad, do we have to go to another cemetery?" Father (Brent) son (Brent II) and a friend (Nick Kanakis) put up a makeshift memorial with their muskets and tricorn hats to honor the grave of the colonel of their historic regiment. Amesbury, MA. Photo by Karen Kemmer.

Members of Col. Bagley's regiment DRESSED FUNNY, posing for mug shots on our unit vacation and sightseeing trip. Fort Stanwix, Rome, NY. Photo by Karen Kemmer.

"Come and get it!" After a week of sightseeing and moteling it, members of our unit rented KOA camp cabins and had an enjoyable barbeque in the rain. Trips like this are great camaraderie builders! Photo by Karen Kemmer.

"Here we go, Dear! Hang on, we're headed for another reenactment." One of our vacations took us to Salem, MA, where we couldn't resist stepping behind this character board. (Authors Karen and Brent Kemmer.) Photo by Brent Kemmer II.

⚜ 6 ⚜

Wife, Prepare Yourself!

If you are not organized,
then your husband had better be!

KAREN: To best prepare yourself, be something that *I* am not: hardworking and very organized! Ever since we first got married, Brent, being a bit of a "type A" personality, has been the chief list-maker and organizer in our family, but believe me, every family can benefit from the innate organizational abilities of a "type A" person! For example, Brent likes to do all the packing, not because he wants to, but because he wants it done *his* way.

A wife should prepare herself when a couple or family enters this hobby because a large amount of the work will fall on her shoulders. This is not to say that your partner will do nothing, but that you will do the sewing, dishes and laundry and help pack, set up and unpack. When our son was little this was the most difficult, but as the years have gone by, things have gotten easier.

✑ "FORT"-IFY YOURSELF!

This hobby can be much more consuming than any other. This does not just mean in time and money but in total absorption of your family life and lifestyle. To give you some examples, when Brent and I started out, we naively thought it

Here it is! This is why we bought our house and property! The dream of many reenactors is to have their own fort. Troops of Ogden's Provincial Rangers, Reid's Company of the 42nd Regiment of Foot and Col. Jonathan Bagley's Regiment regularly enjoy weekends at Fort Bagley on the Kemmers' acreage in Houghton Lake, MI. Fort Bagley has a 20-man barracks within its stockade. A nice area has also been made for French and Indian camping on the other side of the woods. Photo by Karen Kemmer.

would be a cool thing to do; just a little camping and dressing in historic clothes. Fortunately or unfortunately (depends on your line of thought) we now own twenty acres of rolling hardwoods because we (Brent) had to have an 18th-century fort, we have a home that is decorated in 18th-century furniture, we have an expensive truck to haul everything, Brent has a den taking up room in the house, we always take vacations planned around living history and Brent talks of nothing else and is constantly writing some articles or manuscripts (and now he even has me doing it). So get ready for the <u>best</u> or worst time of your life!

✏ HELPFUL TIPS FOR WIVES

(1) Make clothes that require little sewing.
(2) Keep kid's clothes simple, loose fitting and un-elaborate.
(3) Use elastic, but hide it well.
(4) Buy or trade for whatever you can't make.
(5) Trade kid's clothes with other reenactor parents rather than make everything.
(6) Cook meals ahead of time.
(7) Have everyone in the family learn how to pack and unpack their own clothes and gear.
(8) Pack ahead of time.
(9) Have the kids help with camp setup. They can fetch tent stakes at an early age.
(10) Take books, games or tapes in your car for travel with kids. We even used to take an AC-DC adapter for long trips and took a TV, VCR and Nintendo.
(11) Teach everyone to do their own laundry, or at least to help with sorting, folding, mending, etc., until they are old enough to be completely responsible for their own outfits (as if that would ever happen).
(12) Always have baby wipes for everyone in your family at camp and in the car.

(13) Limit the kids' drinks (and yours) near bedtime so you don't hear, "Mom, can you walk me to the port-a-potty?" in the middle of the night!

(14) Pay close attention to the weather reports and pack accordingly.

(15) Make sure you have good directions (this can cause the biggest arguments).

(16) Make sure you give someone a phone number or address where you'll be camping and an itinerary.

(17) Last, but not least, enjoy your weekend!

✍ TAKING OVER YOUR LIFE

Here, there, everywhere.
You'll eat it, sleep it and even drink it!

When we first got into reenacting, people used to tell me that their whole house was filled with reenacting items. Oh, I thought, that would never happen to me; no hobby would ever take over my life! Well, twenty years later I can tell you, I have colonial items in every room in our home.

 Brent loves to decorate. In the late 70's and early 80's he was the showroom manager of a large, expensive furniture design studio. One of his duties was to work with and check the paperwork of over a dozen interior decorators, and I guess some of their ideas and talents rubbed off. We have decorated our home in a colonial manner without giving it that "museum look." Everything from fabrics and furniture styles to lighting and accessories are as authentic as possible.

Some reenacting items make great decorating accents. For instance, a tricorn hat and 18th-century saddlebags draped over an old ladder back chair can warm up an otherwise empty corner. I would like to give you some ideas of what we have done with our house. Blue and wine-colored hand-blown glassware collections from Colonial Williamsburg adorn the windowsills in our dining room. In our bedroom we have a four-post bed with canopy and drapes. On the posts hang a white powdered wig and another tricorn. We also have a chamber pot and bed warmer in our bedroom. One of our nicest pieces of furniture is in this room. It is a New England reproduction pine highboy. Our pride and joy is our sofa. It is a Chippendale camelback sofa with a crewel tapestry for fabric.

We also have several painted and unpainted chests and boxes that help with storage. They look great and are functional, too.

Just remember, don't pile all your reenacting gear all over, making it look like junk! You have spent great deal of time and money on this stuff. By having it around as accessories it tells your guests a little about your interesting hobby (in our case, a *lot* about it)! You can also hang clothes on the walls from pegs, hooks or handmade nails. A woman's gown on a dress form would also look great, and people would always come away inspired.

Our house has even taken on the character of our reenacted time period. Pictured is our pride and joy, our camelback Chippendale sofa (off limits to the dog, Brent's feet and anyone with a speck of dirt on them!). Photo by Brent Kemmer.

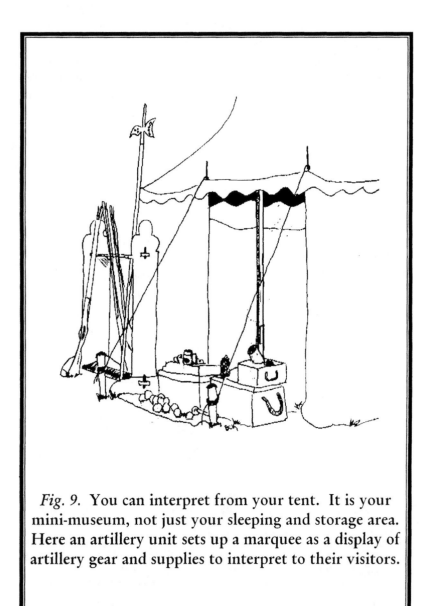

Fig. 9. You can interpret from your tent. It is your mini-museum, not just your sleeping and storage area. Here an artillery unit sets up a marquee as a display of artillery gear and supplies to interpret to their visitors.

❦ 7 ❧

Camp Life

*In the daytime you're under the scrutiny of the public eye,
but "after hours" a special magic begins!*

Much of your time as a living historian will be spent talking
to the public or putting on demonstrations. This is really what
we do living history for—or *is* it? Once you take part in a
living history encampment or event you will be hooked. This
may be because of the personal gratification you get from
teaching the public about our heritage. It also may be because
of the fun you have after hours around the campfire with the
other living historians. Regardless of *why* you enjoy your
hobby, it is inevitable that you are out for the best times in
your life!

❧ WELCOME TO MY TENT

The camp life that you demonstrate to visitors is a key element
of historical interpretation. By setting up an encampment, be
it a Medieval fair or a Vietnam War American soldier's bush
camp, you are inviting the public into your home—your home
for that weekend, at least. This is a very personal invitation by
you for their learning, and of course for your pleasure.

Your camp provides a proper backdrop for the event. We
are not always lucky enough to have a historic site as our
location. The inside of your camps are also mini-museums, so

set them up for viewing. With this proper setting you now are ready to perform the interpreting that we discussed earlier. Enjoy talking and demonstrating to your public, and prepare for enjoyment after they are gone, as well.

✍ To Cook, Or Not To Cook

One of the best interpretations is the preparation of food.
Use it as a demonstration and as a stimulation
to expand into other teaching.

Now that you have a proper setting, you need to be *doing* something. Your historic counterparts didn't just sit around. Soldiers weren't in battle during an entire campaign. One of the most time consuming daily chores for civilians and military alike was, and is, food preparation. Show how and what your character ate in his period. As with all your living history, make sure you have done your research first, you never want to lead the public astray.

A good example of colonial food preparation can be demonstrated with the help of documentation found in military records. The soldiers we portray were issued bread or flour, beef or pork, rice, peas or beans, meal, molasses, ginger, sugar, butter and rum. If in garrison they were expected to have gardens to supplement these rationed foods. They also had sutlers who followed the regiments and sold additional foods. Some of these supplements were milk, eggs, beets, potatoes, poultry, vinegar, fish, vegetables, tea, chocolate, strawberries, cider, apples and beer. Officers additionally had much more varied food coffers to draw from.

Using the staple rations for a soldier, you could prepare a proper meal in proper containers in front of the public. Take your meat, rice, peas, butter, water and a touch of flour; place it all in your tin mess kettle and put it over the fire to boil. When it comes to a boil, put it to the side of the coals and let it simmer. Stir it so it doesn't burn, and when the rice is done you have a ration stew. Eat hardy with some butter on your bread and a little rum in your water to drink, and you're eating as a colonial soldier did—*if* you were lucky enough to get full rations (yum, yum).

If you're demonstrating authentic period cooking in front of the public, use the foods we can document and use the utensils they were issued. Be creative and make variations with your rations and any supplemental foods you could have purchased, killed or grown. If you're not cooking for a demonstration then do what you want, but don't tell the public, "This is what they ate," if you're having macaroni and cheese.

━◆◆━

KAREN: There is nothing that says or regulates that you *must* cook at camp. When the weather is cool I find it warming to work over the fire. It also gives ladies something to do around camp while the men (soldiers) are off fighting or drilling. Cooking also is one of the best "rope line" tools for leading the public into your interpretation.

At many events, some of the rations (fixings) or meals are provided for the participants. Sometimes these rations are authentic and can be used in front of the public. You may want to supplement your own foods them with. Sometimes the food is not even close to being authentic, but that usually takes place at large events that are very busy, and it is not rationed out in front of the public, so who cares? It's food, and you don't have to cook it!

Another option that our unit enjoys at far away events is going out to eat. Sometimes it's just too hot, and everyone has worked so hard during the day that you and the family just need to get away, get into some air conditioning and relax. This is a wonderful way to deepen camaraderie amongst your unit as well. And don't forget, with little ones tugging at your skirts all day it takes a lot more effort and time to cook over a fire than it does at home, and these events may be the only "vacations" that you will take. The choice is often up to you, to cook or not to cook, that is the question.

We're hungry!

BRENT: Karen and another woman were cooking together a few years ago at an encampment where we were furnished with chickens and vegetables and other fixings. They took the fixings and vegetables and made a stew, and then started to clean and prepare the chickens. A few people were walking through the camp, but nobody was paying much attention to the women cooking.

Being true comedians and wanting to show off their hard work, Karen and the other woman started an impromptu argument. They began throwing insults at each other (keeping in their colonial character, of course). As the quarrel escalated, a small crowd gathered around. The two (ladies?) each grabbed an end of a large chicken and began pulling, and then began comparing each other's husbands to the chicken's body parts. This went on for several minutes as the onlookers enjoyed the spectacle. By the end of the argument Karen and her friend had their complete attention, and were able to draw them into the setting and share their knowledge of 18th-century food and its preparation.

✑ THEY ASK THE STRANGEST QUESTIONS

"They didn't have canvas back then!"

Shortly after Karen and her friend got done tugging on that chicken, they placed it on a spit over the fire and began roasting it slowly. A man walked by with his son and stopped to look at the cooking bird. He bent over and said to his boy, "Look, son, it's wax. See it dripping?" Obviously, he had never cooked a meal in his life; chickens do drip fat when they are roasted!

I hate to say that any question is stupid. As educators we love our students to ask questions. This is one of the best ways to tell if your students are learning and enthused about what you're teaching. But some of the questions that we have gotten over the years at camp really take the cake!

Here are some amusing questions and comments we have heard over the years:

* Do you really sleep in those tents?
* They didn't have canvas back then!
* Do those guns really shoot?
* Are you warm in those clothes?
* Look son, those people aren't really sleeping, they're pretending!
* Do you fire real bullets at each other?
* How much do you get paid to do this?
* They only had white and black wool back then!
* You made that in the microwave in your tent!
* Oh, so you have a cooler!
* Is that what people really wore or are you just making it up?
* Why are you drinking out of a metal cup?

And the all-time winner goes to a woman who walked by with her son, knelt down and as she reached into our fire pit told him,

* "It's not a real fire! OUCH!!!"

✑ COME GATHER 'ROUND THE FIRE

*A true fondness, friendship, and fellowship
exists among living historians; a fraternal outward sharing
not felt to this extent elsewhere.*

Although there are a few who go it alone in this hobby, it is
really a team activity as well as a social gathering. You wait
with anticipation for the next weekend's camp. From the
minute you arrive, you look for the others of your unit or
organization. Everyone chips in and helps put up the camp,
and conversations begin. Once the camp is up, at least in our
unit, we get changed into our period clothing and shed the
21st century—we prefer to stay in period clothing for the
entire event. A fire pit is dug, the fire is lit, and chairs and
stools are dragged over to its inviting glow. It can be 90
degrees out, but we still congregate by that fire. Then through
the entire event we are together, as brothers and sisters,
working as a unit, shopping together, drilling, fighting,
cooking (or going out to eat), and looking out for each other.
Even at the end of an event, no matter how tired or eager you
may be to go back to the 21st century, you still have an empty
feeling for leaving your "family" till the next event.

This is a feeling that you and your unit must foster. If you
truly want to achieve a cohesive unit of "friends," you must
continually work together to better your unit. This is an
ancient idea, and just as it is in our reenacting, the true
militaries of our heritage have prided themselves with this
esprit de corps. For years men have been drawn into units
noble and proud. Their uniforms, banners and honors hold
them together as a most cohesive unit. So too, even in our
living history as we strive to portray our historical
counterparts, we also develop this true camaraderie which,
when blended with our quest for uniformity, produces our
esprit de corps.

Not only do the men in our group feel this passion, but the ladies of the unit also join together in the true quest of friendship and living history. A good example was when our unit's ladies decided to sew cross-stitch squares. All summer they took their squares to camp and worked on them together. Many worked on them at home as well. Then they added some regimental insignias and sewed them into quilts. At our holiday party we raffled them off for superb door prizes!

Even away from the weekends, the camaraderie is kept up through parties, meetings and newsletters. Parties are becoming quite popular now with units, but not too long ago there were few. Our unit has an annual holiday party where we dress in our period uniforms and have a great feast together. Many units have monthly meetings and work sessions where they go over how they want things to run, and work together to make parts of their uniform and gear. Quite a few units have newsletters to keep their members informed. These newsletters may be issued monthly, quarterly or annually. Many of them are becoming very elaborate and professional looking thanks to modern computer software.

⚜ 8 ⚜

Selecting A Unit
Or Going It Alone

—⚜—

*This is one of the most serious decisions you will make in
reenacting. Make your selection wisely,
base it on personality, personality, personality!*

Are you going to attend living history events by yourself or
are you going to join a unit? Are you going to participate by
yourself or are you participating with your family or a friend?
These are important questions that only you can answer, but
they are only the beginning of the questions you should be
asking yourself and prospective units before you jump aboard!
As we stated earlier, to us this is a group effort. There are
a few individuals who go to living history weekends alone, but
there are numerous reasons for joining a group or unit. When
looking for a unit to join, there are some recommendations we
have for you. We have been members of several different time
periods and have belonged to ten living history units and
three different umbrella organizations through the years.
They have not all been the best of our experiences but some
have been very special to us. Consequently, our experiences
led us to the following list of questions you should ask
yourself and a prospective units.

Things to ask yourself:

(1) Do I/we want to join a unit?
(2) Do I/we want a unit that is a dictatorship, democracy, or oligarchy?
(3) Would I/we be better suited to run our own unit?
(4) Do I/we want a very strict unit?
(5) Do I/we want some latitude with clothing and gear?
(6) How important is authenticity to me/us?
(7) Where is the unit based?
(8) Where are unit's events from my home?

Things to ask prospective units:

(1) How do I/we join?
(2) Are you a family oriented unit?
(3) Can individuals join?
(4) Can women belong or is this unit for men only?
(5) If women are allowed to join, do they actively take part in events and activities?
(6) Do you have dues?
(7) Are you affiliated with any other units or organizations?
(8) What type of research has your unit done?
(9) Do you require minimum standards of knowledge, education, attendance, etc., for members?
(10) Do you have a list of unit rules?
(11) Do you have safety rules?
(12) If military, how do you promote?
(13) Do you allow members to make decisions?
(14) Who is the leader of your unit?
(15) What is there for women to do?
(16) Are members required to have certain items of historical clothing and gear? If so, what are those items?
(17) How many meetings do you have?

(18) Where are your events, how many are there and which are required?
(19) When can kids take part in activities?
(20) Do you have any parties or other fun activities?
(21) Do you have a newsletter?
(22) Do you have other forms of communication?
(23) Do you allow drinking, and if so, how much?
(24) What do you want new members to know about your unit?

After you have met with the representatives of a prospective unit or units, ask other living historians about the unit you are thinking of joining. This is an important decision, and if it doesn't work out, it can cost you a lot of time, money and grief.

Every unit has a personality, just as individuals do. You want to make sure your personality, or your family's personality, will fit with that of the unit. For instance, you don't want to join an all-male unit that travels long distances and parties heavily if you are joining as a family who is quite religious. On the other hand, you don't want to join a group of less-than-authentic families who pack too much and sit around and talk about their babies' first steps if you're a single guy who has no intention of ever marrying, wants to do living history as authentically as possible and wants to drink a few beers around the camp fire in the evening.

We have found over the years units that are family oriented, those that prefer singles, partiers, authenticity nuts, units who have the idea that "if they'd had it they'd have used it," units that mix modern with period ideas creating some kind of giant anachronism, loners, battle-enthusiastic units, those who sit around the rope lines and never budge from the spot, units that are afraid to talk to the public, drunks, units that actively steal members from other units, units that just couldn't care less about anything except dressing up, groups that do no research at all and units that are well-rounded living historians.

This is one reason that we as a family bounced around for a few years, trying to find a unit with the correct personality for us. We were in many good units and a few that were a real mistake. Finally, we looked at our own personal interests, what we wanted to get out of living history, and what we were being offered, and we decided to form our own group. Don't think that this is the right decision for you. It takes eight hours a day to run and organize a unit the correct way, and if you're not that devoted then you will not succeed!

You will also run into units that will actively try to recruit you. These units often will have many questions for you as well. Just keep in mind the fact that they have a reputation to uphold and standards to adhere to within their group. And many commanders consider their units their personal empires. (Sorry, but we do.)

We don't recommend recruiting to all units. You need to be very organized (that's where Brent comes in, he's a "type A" personality, you know).

The key is doing your research (here we go again) on which units do what, and what they're really like. It's your time and money so ask questions.

∽ YOU'RE IN THE ARMY NOW!

You enlisted and whether you like it or not,
you are expected to perform in a military fashion at all times.
DO YOU UNDERSTAND?

BRENT: If you are now a recruited reenactor, you are part of this elite military called weekend warriors. (And you thought the National Guard was the only one, didn't you!) Military reenactors are my "brethren." I never served in the real military but I have a deep respect for all who have. All the reenactors I have met have this same patriotic passion for the men and women who made us what we are today. We owe them the deepest and sincerest honor by representing them through our living history. It is also our duty to portray our historic friends with as much accuracy as possible. (You must forgive my preaching in this small but important section.) It is because of this passion that I say, "If you're portraying military, then *be* military, or get out!"

We are attempting to educate the public on the often delicate subject matter of their fallen relatives. Additionally, we are trying to stimulate people to seek further knowledge about our military history. The only way to do this as reenactors is to be the best damned military units possible. Now don't get me wrong, I don't feel that we need to flog every man who gets out of line or keelhaul men for not following orders, or even hang a man for walking off the field of battle. We are not "real military." But we are representing men and women who were, and we must do our best to represent them authentically.

There are going to be times when you're not going to feel like playing army, or you are sick or it's too hot. That can be understandable and overlooked if you're not out in front of your public. What I am recommending, though, is that to the utmost of your ability you and your unit have the appearance of a military unit. Wear the uniforms proudly, stand erect and march in step. If you are part of an elite unit, such as the grenadiers and lights in the colonial British army, then stand taller and fight harder than the rest. If you are portraying Robert Rogers' Rangers, then you know from your research that you were not only be the best in the woods warfare, but also you had to be the best at all military skills.

No matter what your military portrayal, you are today as yesterday under a chain of command, and in front of the public you should never deviate from it. Set your camps up correctly, practice your manual of arms, and above all, have a soldierly air about your every movement. Of course, when the public is gone you can let your hair down (some of us more than others). This is true, at least, if you are not doing a total 24-hour experimental archaeological test of military etiquette.

So if you're in a military reenactment group, that means you're in the army. If you're in the army, then you need to act like it, if not for your unit, then for the public, and above all for those you are portraying and who lost their lives for you and your country!

If you want to attend one of the largest events, and by far the largest encampments in North America, go to the annual Grand Encampment at Fort Ticonderoga in Ticonderoga, NY. On the left are provincial and Ranger mess camps and flies across the military street from the soldier's tents. (Foreground, author Brent Kemmer, Larry Aiello.) Photo by Karen Kemmer.

✿ 9 ✿

Selecting & Planning Events

—✿✿✿✿✿—

*Every weekend, there are at least four living history events
to select from. Make your selection carefully!*

KAREN: If I have to be completely honest about how I go
about selecting an event, I look at what conveniences and
comforts are offered there or nearby. Here is a list of what I
look for when selecting which events to attend.

* Showers on site or nearby.
* Real flush toilets in clean bathrooms.
* Coffee/tea in the morning.
* Continental type breakfast (fruit, donuts, bagels).
* A lunch or dinner furnished (stew or bean soup means
    we're going out).
* A building on site to get out of the weather.
* Medical help on site.
* A pool or playground to take the kids to when they get
    bored.
* Good motels or hotels nearby.
* Good restaurants nearby.
* Phones on site.
* Security on site 24 hours a day.
* Sites or attractions close by, to take mini sightseeing
    trips.
* Ice on site.

This doesn't mean that if an event is out in the middle of nowhere I won't go to it, it just means I'll need a little more convincing. Most events have some of the items on my list and some have all of them. I'm also careful to go camping only from the last of May through the end of September. The weather in and around Michigan is too iffy for me before and after those dates. I'm not going to a camp and be cold and wet; it just won't be enjoyable enough. (And we all know if *I'm* not happy I'll make sure Brent's not happy!) If I were going with Brent after or before those dates I'd prefer a motel.

BRENT: My ideas for selecting an event are in some ways the same as Karen's, but in others, different. I imagine this is partially because I'm also looking at it from my unit's concern, not just my family. Here is my list.

* Good ground for camping.
* Good ground for battling.
* Enjoyable battles.
* Security.
* Ample toilet facilities that are kept CLEAN.
* Good dry split firewood.
* Ice.
* Organization.
* Safety.
* On an historical site.
* Barracks space so we don't have to camp.
* Was my unit utilized properly and to our best abilities?
* Do sponsors or organizers have a good enough understanding of the war and in particular our unit?
* Is it always a poor weather weekend?

These are some of the major things that I look for when I select an event. I don't have to have all of them, but I also can live with more amenities like modern toilets, meals, coffee in the morning, things for the wives and kids and places to go out and eat. I look at all the event possibilities, not just the fair weather times of the year. I actually prefer spring, winter and fall events.

Obviously, this gives you different ways of looking at events. These are personal choices that you and or your family and unit will have to make. There is no way we can make them for you, but you can use these ideas as guidelines as you start looking for events to attend. Sometimes our unit sends men only to a new event, to find out if it's a place we want to take our families. It has paid off several times! Also, keep in mind the best place to look for events is *Smoke and Fire News* (See Appendix 2).

KAREN: We have had many experiences with events over the last twenty years, and it's hard to select our favorite, but some of them are more memorable than others. Several years ago, when Brent II was only about eight years old, we went to the first Fort Ticonderoga event. Brent helped put this event on with a friend from Michigan and a guy from New York. It was quite an experience, not just because of the challenges of organizing a large event, but also because of the distance from our home and because we made it our base camp for ten days, sleeping on straw for the entire time. (We found out why they aired their tents. Even though we showered daily, our tent began to smell like a barnyard)!

Speaking of barnyards, at that time they still allowed cows to graze in the adjacent field. One morning the cows got loose and got into our encampment! I hid in the tent and screamed. Some of the men came to my rescue and drove them away at bayonet point (they were thrilled to have finally used them for something).

During this long ten-day encampment, we ladies got rather tired of the whole reenacting thing! One day an older gentleman and his wife mentioned they were going to Burlington, Vermont, for the day and wanted to know if any of us wanted to accompany them. Well you'd have thought the cows had stampeded again because we took off at a dead run for his van! I often like to take side trips like this. After all, it's *our* vacation too!

Also, while at this same encampment the men were determined to climb "Rogers' Rock." We ladies stayed in camp and cooked for everyone. We told the boys, "Go for it!" It was over 90 degrees that day and they went in full marching kits and uniforms! About one o'clock we could hear guns firing way off in the distance towards Rogers' Rock. We knew they had made it to the top; it was their signal! A couple of hours later their van pulled in, the doors slowly opened and the boys slowly emerged. Brent took the cake, though—he was crawling on his hands and knees! They had made it, but HOW they did pay! At least they can say that they did it, and in full uniform and gear!

❖❖❖

✑ How to Put on an Event

Be ready for a lot of work, little thanks
and a test of your organizational skills.

There are several schools of thought when it comes to putting
on an event. One would be that you have a large committee to
organize and make all arrangements. The second would be to
keep your committee small so not to be overwhelmed with too
many personalities. A third idea would be to run an event
totally on your own. And for some reason, some people think
that events will run themselves: WRONG!

The suggestions we offer here should give you a good idea
of what to do to be successful. The way you organize your
event is going to depend on the size of the event, whether it's
the first time for the event, and what is to be accomplished at
the event.

The first thing you'll need to do is decide what you want
to accomplish at your event and how large you want it to be.
Ask yourself, "What do I want to accomplish: a primitive
event, a battle festival, a trade fair, a rope line demonstration
or an event at a historic site?" When working with the size of
your event you may run up against things such as: your site
might not be large enough, the date might not work well with
other events, the time of year may be bad for many people to
attend or you may not have the things that really draw big
numbers.

No matter what answer you arrive at for the size and what you want to accomplish, there are some key things to keep in mind.

* Keep things organized.
* Have everything OK'd by the site.
* Make sure participants enjoy themselves.
* Make sure to invite people and units that do your kind of event.
* Publicize your event.
* Make sure invitations are precise and include times and good directions.
* Make sure the amenities you promised are on site and in good condition.
* Enlist others you can depend on to help you or your committee.

To give you an example, let's look at a small rope line demonstration event first. We recommend that you organize these types of events by yourself or with a small group. With small events, large organizing groups will be too overwhelming.

First, you need to sit down with the event sponsor and see what moneys are available for mailings, advertising, amenities, etc. The next thing you'll need to do is create a schedule of events that you wish to take place. At small events you need to keep people busy, but not *too* busy (See Appendix 7). There are not many things for participants to do on their own at small events, so give them a moderate schedule. This schedule will also give the public a listing of things they can watch or participate in throughout their day of visiting. Now sit down and come up with a list of participants to invite, draft the actual invitation and send it out.

Next, make a list of everything that will need to be done before, during and after the event. Be very detailed, and if you enlist help, delegate jobs; there's nothing that says *you* have to do it all! You will need to decide things like whether or not to offer meals, and if so, who will pick them up or cook them. If you run game-type events, what will the prizes be? Who will be in charge during the event? Who is in charge of camp setup? Who is going to get the wood, water and porta-potties on site? How often will the porta-potties be emptied? How will you make announcements if needed? Who will do the advertising? And the list goes on and on and on.

Looking at much larger events, we recommend that you definitely have a committee to help; just keep the committee down to manageable size. You'll start out the same, deciding what you want to accomplish and what size of an event to have.

Let's say you want a 500 to 1000 participant reenactment with two battles on Saturday and one on Sunday. We recommend that after you arrive at a list of participants to invite, send out unit invitations rather than individual ones. There is much less paperwork and much less expense. You also might want to consider sending as many invitations as possible over the Internet. Be very insistent, though, about having updates on numbers of participants and tentage the week before the actual event. (This also can be done easily over the Internet.)

Then you proceed by developing a schedule. At larger reenactments you don't need as full of a schedule as at small events. Many sutlers or merchants often set up at larger events, giving reenactors something to do on their off time. (Sutlers and merchants are another group that you should consider inviting for a well-rounded event.) Also, if you're doing several battles a day, the reenactors will need some down time to recuperate. There usually are other items of a military nature such as flag ceremonies and officers' calls to fill up the schedule (See Appendix 8).

Now, have your committee brainstorm everything that will need to be done before, during and after the event, and *delegate* the jobs—you won't be able to do it all! You will need experts on all aspects of the event, i.e., camp setup, food prep, period flag ceremonies, battle safety and tactics, etc. You will

also need to develop a full chain of command and let everyone
know from the get go what it is and that it is to be followed.
Reenactments are military and reenactors respond best to
military organizing.

We'd like to use two events that we helped put on as
examples. The first was a small rope line demonstration and
reenactment in Mt. Pleasant, Michigan several years ago. This
proved to be a very enjoyable event. We ran it ourselves with a
very small committee of four. We did enlist the university
museum and the city Chamber of Commerce to help with
financing.

We sat down with the city and told them what we wanted
to accomplish, our dates, and the expected costs. They gave us
the OK and we got started. We acquired a list of participants
from several other event sponsors and weeded out those that
we believed wouldn't fit in and added others that weren't on
the list. Then we drafted an invitation and mailed it with our
schedule of daily events. We asked people to demonstrate and
talk to visitors all day as well as take part in game-type
activities, take part in flag ceremonies and a battle each day.
We even got the parks people to drag some huge fallen trees
into the middle of the park to create a better aesthetic look for
our battleground. We offered coffee and donuts for breakfast,
free ice, dry oak firewood and soft drinks, and a meal for the
participants. We had porta-potties brought in with orders to
be emptied before breakfast and after supper each day.

Prior to the weekend we took the money donated by the
chamber to sutlers and merchants and purchased prizes for the
daily events. We also wanted to make sure participants
understood we wanted authenticity, so we asked a friend of
ours who was on our committee to make dioramas with lead
figures for prizes. These were given to individuals and camp
setups that our committee thought were outstanding (i.e., best
period outfits and most authentic camps). With our small
committee, the event ran very smoothly.

BRENT: On the other hand, I helped run a larger event this past year at Fort Meigs in Perrysburg, Ohio. A new organization had formed with our organization, "The British Military Family" (the organization of British, provincial and allied reenactors of Michigan), and wanted to put on a large "Grand Encampment" at different sites around the country. A young man from Wisconsin did a lot of preliminary work contacting and recruiting units to participate. The idea was to have a VERY militarily run, properly set up, French and Indian War event with large sized battles. I was asked by the site to be the British field commander.

I started by organizing a chain of command, four months before the actual event. I placed three men as commanders of the three divisions, one in charge of grenadiers and regulars, one in charge of provincials, lights and rangers, and one in charge of artillery and horse. Each of these men had a major under them in charge of each subdivision and each major had subordinate officers appointed to them. Each subdivision as well had appointed non-commissioned officers to run the units.

We set up a command headquarters in one of the blockhouses and ran our army with full military etiquette during the entire encampment. We also asked all participants to consciously restrict their camp furniture to be as Spartan as they could.

I was in contact with the site and my commanders weekly, and daily in the last two weeks before the event. The Internet made this very easy. We also insisted that units keep us abreast on their numbers and camps up until the night before the event, so we were able to set up our camp very authentically, with very few holes in our streets. This camp also was a little different, because the site was in charge of the event, and I only had the British army in my charge. The French were run similarly but separately, consequently we didn't have to deal with food, porta-potties, firewood, water, invitations and other amenities.

Here are some ideas for planning any successful event:
* Organize!
* Have 24-hour security.
* Have medical people on site or very close.
* Be in contact with sponsors.
* Be in contact with invited units.
* Have amenities on site and functional.
* Offer food or meals.
* Have enough on the daily schedule but not too much.
* Set up your camp accurately.
* Have setup times during the day and evening before the event starts.
* Close the event to the public Sundays between 2 and 4 p.m. so participants can make it home at a decent time.
* Don't let your event get stagnant, try new things.
* Have activities for the whole family.
* Have a good working safety program.

Don't make the following mistakes that we have seen at too many events:

Let your porta-potties overflow; don't keep toilet paper in the porta-potties; have nothing for participants to do; have too much for participants to do; have no security in a bad area; don't have enough wood; run out of water; run out of food; make participants stand around in the sun while you figure out what to do; invite reenactors and not have a battle; have very lame battle scenarios.

✍ How To Lay Out A Camp

*Take time and effort in your event's camp setup, it's the
first line of interpretation. Having a well laid out camp will
make the participants feel more authentic as well.*

Through the ages military camps have had uniformity in their
setup. One can look at diagrams of the earliest camps and see a
structure aligning warriors and leaders. Scholars have studied
the art of castramentation (selecting, measuring and placing
camps in order) since the beginnings of warfare. No matter
what time period you are recreating, with research you will
find the proper camp setup. We recommend that you do this
research and set your camps up as properly as possible. By
doing so your camps will be safer, more authentic and easier
for the public to understand. It makes your encampment the
ultimate canvas museum!

As an example of a proper camp setup for the British army
during the French and Indian War, reenactors can use
Humphrey Bland's *Treatise of Military Discipline*. In his 1759
edition he shows a camp plan for an encampment of a
battalion of 630 soldiers. His plan stretches a length of 320
yards from quarter guard to rear guard. At this time in living
history, we of the French and Indian War era don't have
events with that many Brits, so we must scale down our
encampments. We can do this and keep with the same
organization, proportionate to our numbers.

Most areas that we are allowed to use are not large enough
for full alignment with military protocol. Bland starts with a
rear guard, then sutlers, and then kitchens. He then places the
officers' tents in a tiered formation starting with the staff
officers, then the highest-ranking officer, and then rows of
subordinate officers. This creates a pyramid effect of officers'
tents. Bland then places the enlisted men's tents in streets by
companies. He also places the sergeants' tents next in line,

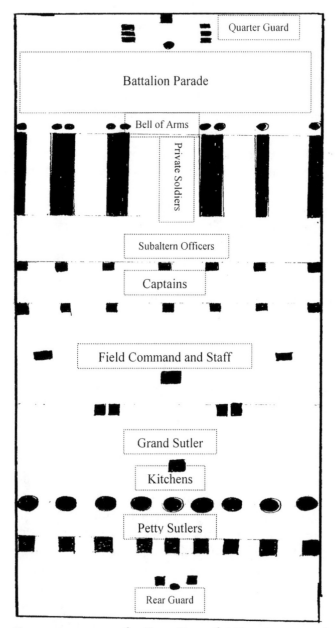

Facsimile encampment of a Battalion of 163 privates and their officers. Taken from "A Treatise of Military Discipline," by Humphrey Bland (London) 1759, p. 292.

facing out to the bells of arms, which face into a parade area. After the parade he places a quarter guard camp.

This would be very difficult for us as reenactors to achieve. First of all, we don't usually have enough camps and men to have a rear and quarter guard and a camp for the army as well. Second, we usually don't have sutlers with our living history units; they are individual business owners rather than attached to units. Third, we are restricted sometimes as to where we can have our fires (kitchens) and how much area we can take up.

When putting together your camp, first draw it out to scale on paper. If it works on paper it will probably work at your site. When you arrive on site, measure or pace off all the sections and streets of your camp. There are two ways to mark off your measurements. You can either use paint or, as we recommend, use small stakes and twine or string as they did historically. With this step complete, and leaving a good person in charge, your camp should set up nicely.

We recommend for public events that you omit the guard camps and sutlers' areas, and start off with the officers' tents. Place them in a tiered arrangement starting with the highest-ranking officer and work your way down the officer chain creating a pyramid, as did Bland. Then put a street dividing officers from the rest of the army. Next, place the sergeants' tents at the head of each company street, facing the subordinate officers' tents. If you have bells of arms, they should be beside the sergeants' tents. Now align your soldiers' tents in company streets facing into each other or out from each other, depending on how many streets you'll need. At the end of the soldiers' tent streets, leave a street and then place the kitchens (company mess tents or flies). This setup, though adaptive from Bland, will still give you a very organized, very authentic and safe camp setup.

Finally, there are several things we recommend you look out for when organizing encampments. Make your streets large enough for cars to go down for ease of loading and unloading (15-20 feet wide). Keep tents away from the kitchen areas for fire safety. Set up your enlisted men's tents as close together as you can to conserve your space and authenticity (stake to stake). Do everything you can to NOT have holes left in the camp. If you plan, you can adapt our suggested layout for any size encampment. And place the person with the most experience in camp set up in charge of this.

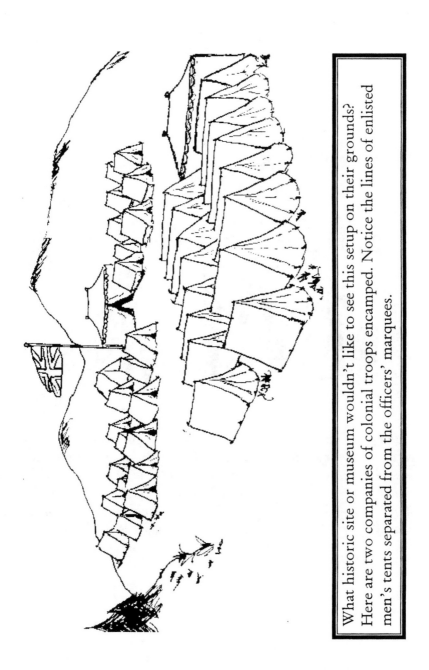

What historic site or museum wouldn't like to see this setup on their grounds? Here are two companies of colonial troops encamped. Notice the lines of enlisted men's tents separated from the officers' marquees.

"Hang on to your hair, Sarg!" One of the main reasons many of us do reenacting is for the fun. We don't know about the sergeant seated in this photo, but the other soldiers sure seem to be enjoying themselves! (Left to right: John Calder, Jeff Makowski, Tim Anderson, Andy Davis, Brent Kemmer II, Dan Kortes; seated center, Sergeant Marv Davis.) Photo by Beth Ignagni.

✍ 10 ✍

Are We Having Fun Yet?

The Unwritten Rules Of Reenacting

—⁓ ⁓ ✳ ⁓ ⁓—

Yes, it's a lot of work, but what hobby worth anything isn't?
Keep yourself in check though, we also do this for fun!

You should be involved quite extensively by now in your new
hobby, and you should be enjoying yourself. With a little
careful planning and attention to detail, these should be some
of the best times of your life. You can meet new people, forget
the hassles of modern life, drift back into a simpler time and
allow yourself to be someone else. This is a rare opportunity
that most people never get to experience.

As we have stated many times now, in order to have the
time and skills to enjoy yourself you must be very organized
and do your research. The amount of time you dedicate to
these key parts of living history will be up to you. Choose
wisely and prepare for a lifetime of enjoyment.

✑ AUTHENTICITY

Make sure you're up to snuff and don't lie to the public.
Most of all, don't lie to yourself.

How authentic should you be? You'll have to make that
decision, unless your unit, if you belong to one, does it for

you. The main guideline that we can offer is that you make yourself educated enough to be believable. The public must feel comfortable with the knowledge that you are sharing with them in order for them to trust you. Do your research and use genuine facts to create a real-looking and real-sounding portrayal for you, your unit and your public.

There are many units and organizations out there in the reenacting community that have very strict guidelines. Some will dictate exactly what you will need and where you must get it. They may also dictate which events you must attend and that everyone in your unit must have the exact same tent. Many others though, don't, and can't dictate such strict regulations. Documentation shows a much wider range of variables for some peoples we represent. Just be careful so that if you join a group that requires strict authenticity, know what they expect from you, and be sure that their requirements are researched to be authentic.

Authenticity doesn't apply only to your clothing and gear. It can also be demonstrated in your speech pattern, the food you eat, and even the way you walk. Just how authentic do you want to be? If you're working as a professional living historian for a historic site, you will have very strict guidelines for the character you are portraying. If you are among the majority of non-paid living historians, you will select your own character and will need to regulate yourself on authenticity.

Whether you decide to develop the portrayal of a *type* of historical person, or of an *actual* character from history, you will need to do much research. We recommend that you create a generic person rather than an actual character from our history. If you try to portray an actual person you will need to know *everything* there is to know about that person or you can't be authentic. You would have to know hundreds of details that there are no way to document. You are much better off if you study the times and create a character that has many similarities to you in your modern life. We have found over the years that if you create a character whose life is too much different from yours, it's extremely difficult to become expert enough on your historic character, and it's too easy to slip out of character and back into the real you. There are several good books that can lead you in your character development (See Appendix 2).

Our experience has shown that those who choose to be blatantly un-authentic will draw everyone's attentions, especially those of other reenactors. They will let you know very quickly what the problems are with your camp, clothing and gear. In some cases you'd swear there are "authenticity police" patrolling an event, and in many instances there may be. Many units and event sponsors place reenactors in charge of checking the authenticity of other reenactors and the encampments at living history events. Some units act as a group or have individuals within the unit to keep up the authenticity levels of their group. There are also individuals who will push the limits of rudeness looking for the tiniest anachronisms, just for the self-gratification that they caught someone. So we recommend that you set levels of authenticity and police yourself. Be as accurate as you can and if you see an anachronism, be polite and point it out, but do it away from the public. This is very important, because the public is much more knowledgeable than many historians think! They often are the first to notice anachronisms, for they are able to stand back and see the whole, rather than just the small part each reenactor portrays.

Years ago, some friends of ours wanted to play a joke on us, and early in the morning before we were awake they snuck over and placed a fluffy garden sheep lawn ornament in front of our tent. Unfortunately, we slept in that morning and, lo and behold, the public was in camp when we awoke. Not only were the other reenactors gathered around outside our tent, but so were several visitors! We never could explain that one to them!

෨ ETHICS

Friends and extended family~
We're all in this together.

One of the nicest aspects that you will notice about this hobby is the fact that everyone stands together. It is one of the unwritten rules of the game that if you're a fellow reenactor, you are part of the brethren and to be treated with respect (for most at least), and help is only a moment away.

In this day and age we see many situations in the world and in our country that are much different than they were when we grew up. Just think how different it is from our historic counterparts' lives! Maybe that is one reason why many of us reenactors feel an overwhelming urge to cling together in this secular fellowship. We often look to the past rather than the future. We continually try and show others the way it used to be in order to help them with the present.

⬗◆⬖

Several years ago we were at an event. We had had a good weekend and the camps were being torn down slowly on a nice Sunday afternoon. All of a sudden several of the ladies of our unit yelled out "Rex needs help!" We thought an army had just been rousted and the battle drums of Caesar had been echoed! There must have been a hundred of us who dropped what we were doing and sprinted from all the corners of camp to where the women pointed us. When we rounded the corner Rex popped out of a porta-pottie where it seems two older teenagers had been trying to tip over that plastic coffin while he was in it! You never saw two men run so fast and jump a fence so high as those two when they saw the rest of us and Rex hot on their heels!

⬗◆⬖

Reenactors have a friendship bond similar to kinship. From the moment we entered reenacting we were brought in, offered food and shelter and welcomed to the campfire. Everyone, no matter what their standing, will help their fellow man within this close knit community. It's as though when we change our clothes our morality changes with them, back possibly to a better time; a time that if not for its hardships, many of us would like to visit.

It is because of this bond that so many of us are drawn to living history. It is the reason that so many of us are bound for life to our hobby. It is a way to show to our fellow reenactors and our visitors how much we care about each other, about them and about our heritage.

BRENT: Years ago this friendship really proved itself to us on our way home from an event at Colonial Michilimackinac. We were driving the old Pontiac Firebird. It was packed to the max with our car top carrier and poles on top, our bedroll and tent on the rear spoiler, and other stuff filling every inch inside, except where Brent II was strapped into his car seat. We were cruising down the expressway reminiscing about our enjoyable weekend, when all of a sudden the temperature gage spun around, the engine clanged several times, I looked in my rear view mirror to see a cloud of white smoke, and the engine quit! What were we going to do? We were an hour and a half from home, with all our gear and a baby! We looked the engine over, hoping it had just overheated, and surveyed the surroundings for signs of a phone or houses (none). We had no money (typical new family). Just then a pickup pulled over. It was a fellow reenactor and his wife! Were we ever happy to see them! They unloaded our stuff into their pickup and all of us piled into the cab and we took off. (We still don't know how we all got inside!) We stopped at the next exit and called for a wrecker to tow the Firebird the next day, and our friends drove us home even though it was about 60 miles out of their way. We've never forgotten their help that day, and to us that is one of the reasons we love reenacting.

﹏ PROFESSIONALISM

Even though we are not paid money for what we do,
we are still professionals.

Even though many living historians don't realize it, they *are* professionals. They are trained specialists who have done much of the research the rest of us take for granted. As many of us like to say, "We pay big bucks to do this." We may not be paid in monetary terms like other professionals are, but we do reap much satisfaction from the entertainment and knowledge we share.

Often we are lucky enough to participate in our living history at historic sites. This can be the ultimate experience for a reenactor: to be on the same ground, to stay in the same barracks, to fight on the same field as our historic counterparts. One thing that we must take into consideration at these sites is that when we are there, we are their employees. Even though we are not getting paid as other interpreters are, we are doing the same job. We are representing not just our historic counterparts but the sites, forts, societies and values of our hosts. It is our responsibility to make sure that we and our units and our organizations are properly and authentically showing the past to the best of our ability. We often are the first line interpreters to the public at these sites on the weekends that we participate. Sometimes we are the only interpreters at a site, and if we are not authentic the public will be misled. As employees and guests of these sites, we as reenactors owe it to these places to act in an ethical, authentic, professional and safe manner at all times.

✍ SAFETY

We must regulate ourselves, or someone else will.

Every year we hear of someone getting badly injured or even killed in our hobby. Fortunately, it has never happened in our French and Indian War time period. This may be partly because we really push safety, or it may be because there are fewer of us. No matter what your time period, we living historians and reenactors must insist on certain safety rules. If you have a unit, if you belong to an organization, or if you are a sponsor, we recommend you develop or adopt a list of rules to govern safety. These rules will not only lead to fewer accidents but also will allow the participants and public to better enjoy the events. Rules of safety also help ensure that there is not an act of neglect.

Safety should never be overlooked as reenactors prepare for battle or any type of firing. Here soldiers stand inspection at The Feast of the Ste. Claire, Port Huron, Michigan. Photo by Karen Kemmer.

Here is an example of a list of safety rules for an event:

* All participants must be registered
* Loads are to be no more than 125 grains of 2Fg or 3Fg black powder
* Muskets must have hammer stalls and flash guards
* All soldiers must have canteens with water
* No original weapons to be fired
* During tacticals all weapons must be elevated above opposing force
* No closing with edged weapons
* Ramrods may NOT be removed from pipes during tacticals
* No hand-to-hand scenarios unless pre-approved by tactical officers
* Participants must be in period clothes while in front of the public
* Military etiquette is in effect at all times
* No pets
* Children are to be under adult supervision at all times
* Fires must be dug in and sod replaced and well watered when leaving
* Fire buckets must be at all fires
* Noise is to be limited after 10 p.m.

The majority of national and regional organizations also have very extensive rules covering weapons, artillery, cavalry, size of charges, ground charges, hand-to-hand combat, edged weapons, tactical safety, inspections, camp safety, fire safety, and etiquette. With these in effect it is also the responsibility of all of us to use common sense at all times. If we are not continually watching for safety and using common sense we are neglectful and cannot sustain a safe environment for our families, sites and our public.

BRENT: When Brent II was only about four or five, I took him by myself to an event. We were doing quite well; I had my fellow soldiers to fight with and he had other kids to play with. After supper I was standing around talking with a few of the guys and Brent and one of his friends were rolling down this little slope, he said later they were pretending to be puppies. All of a sudden I glanced over at him again and he rolled through the fire pit! Talk about scaring the hell out of ya! I ran over and picked up the fire bucket and threw it on his arm (that was all that looked like it was burning). People came running from all over that camp with water and ice. Fortunately, the fire was just smoldering and he moved over it very quickly. The fire did burn through his shirt though and left three small burns on his elbow. We were lucky we thought quickly, with common sense and had safety items on hand. (Surprisingly, Karen didn't kill me when I got home).

The MANUAL EXERCISE *of the* FOOT GUARDS.

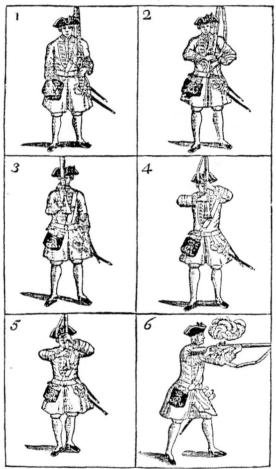

1 Take Care.   2 Join your Right-Hand to your Firelock.   3 Poife your Firelock.
4 Join your Left-Hand to your Firelock.   5 Cock your Firelock.   6 Prefent.   Fire.

❧ Conclusion ❧

Will You Make The Commitment?

—⌁⌁⌁✳⌁⌁⌁—

Now that you have made your choices, you have many benefits to reap from your new life as a historic reenactor!

Well, if we haven't scared you off by now, then you might be reenactor material. In summing things up here, we should point out that this is a hobby where you and your family will continually be involved and growing in many ways, almost too numerous to mention.

You and your family will have fun, meet a wide variety of people from every walk of life and travel and see interesting sites. Everyone who enters this hobby (obsession in our case) gets something different out of it. We asked each other when we were finishing our book, "What has reenacting meant to you?" We also asked our son, who was home for the weekend from college; after all, it has been a family thing for all these years. This is what reenacting has meant to us.

KAREN: If I had to sum up what reenacting has meant to me over the years, or why we put ourselves to so, *SO* much work, I don't think I could tell you in words. Perhaps I can share it best through a treasured memory.

It was in New York at Fort Ticonderoga, overlooking beautiful Lake Champlain. We had been camping on site for several days. We had caravanned there from Michigan with five other families. There had been several military ceremonies and the site was wonderful but I had never been too impressed with any of that, it just didn't grab at me like it did some people. On this particular evening we women had just finished cooking all day and the men had climbed Rogers' Rock as well. After the meal which had fed some twenty of us, one of the staff of the fort who had been hanging around our camp every chance he got wanted to thank us, not just for the meal but for "bringing the grounds to life," as he put it. He climbed to the top of the ramparts of the fort, filled his bagpipes with air and played "Amazing Grace" as the sun slowly set.

We were all listening, my son, husband and myself all deep in our thoughts; a family together in this place filled with history. I could imagine that only a handful of people in our history had stood on that ground where so many had died so long ago and listened to the distant drone of the pipes as the exhausted soldiers were encouraged to fight on. It was a surreal moment for me. Is there another hobby where you can stand on hallowed ground with your family and not only learn and listen to the past, but at times *feel* it? It's as though the voices from the past reach out to us sometimes and say; "Don't forget us, what we have learned, where we came from, how we died building a land for ourselves and for all the generations that will come."

When the past reaches out to us it must be begging to tell the story of our heritage. We should tell all parts as factually as we can, to help educate those who may only seek historical enlightenment to kill an afternoon. This is what we do.

❖❖❖

BRENT II: During the writing of this book my parents posed a question to me. They asked, "What has reenacting meant to you and how it has affected your life?" To answer this question I first have to tell you something. I have never experienced life without reenacting. As long as I can remember my parents and I have done it. I could not imagine what life would be like without all of the experiences it has given me. Because my parents got me involved in reenacting, I now have an unparalleled love for history. Even though I am studying engineering at college, I still think of history every day. History is just something that comes naturally to me.

I remember once when I was very young (about five), I was sitting around the campfire with my dad and some of his friends. As they do at most reenactments, they were talking about some sort of historical event; in this case it was the French Revolution. The content of the conversation was primarily B.S., which is heard quite often at talks around these campfires. Towards the end of the conversation my dad and his friends got into an argument about the year the revolution began. I then out of the blue said, "seventeen eighty-nine." All of the men looked at me as if I were possessed. It was 1789 when the fall of the Bastille started the revolution. Somehow, even at the age of five, reenacting had given me knowledge which these middle-aged men did not possess (at least that night).

Reenacting has not been just a learning experience for me. It has also been a lot of fun. Most of my friends are reenactors. Their ages range from eleven to seventy. I have traveled the country in the pursuit of history. I have visited more graveyards than I would like to admit. I have portrayed a

French *voyageur*, Native American, Rogers' Ranger, Scottish Highlander, 3rd Massachusetts Provincial and 10th Royal Veteran. I have held the rank/status of camp follower, centinel (private), drummer, surgeon's mate assistant, corporal, sergeant, ensign, and lieutenant. I am on the board of our living history organization. I have been told what to do and I have told others what to do. I have become extremely proficient at the manual arms drill. I can load and fire my musket 6-8 times in a minute. I built three cannons in high school metal shop, one of which is a full size light three-pounder.

None of my non-reenacting friends have done these things, which makes me different from all of those friends. However, I am proud to be different, and I am proud to hold the title of "REENACTOR!"

◆◆◆

BRENT: Digging deep within, it was very difficult to come up with what reenacting has truly meant to me. It has been so very much.

During my childhood when my family went on vacation, we would sometimes visit historic sites, but these were considered side trips; they were not the actual goal of the trip. I have not really taken my own family on vacations *per se*, but rather on site seeking weeks and weekends where we concentrated on history, research or living history, and sometimes we may have spent some time in a pool or something for relaxation. In this respect, perhaps I have failed to take them on a "real" vacation. But when I look at the other things that I have experienced I am glad and proud.

Reenacting has made a huge impact on my life by offering opportunities not available to me otherwise, and by providing a portal through which I semi-monthly leave the 21st century for the 18th century. In my daily life I am a full-time middle school history teacher and periodically I am on the adjunct teaching staff at our local community college. It is not a glamorous life—quite common, in fact—offering little advancement or appreciation. I am a somewhat ordinary husband, father, committee member and middle class worker. Through my living history I have been able to advance in ranks, start my own unit, and offer my assistance to several national organizations in various representative positions. After getting quite involved in our hobby I was taken by the writing bug and now have authored 6 non-fiction books, one fiction work and numerous articles. I am also lucky enough to be the current French and Indian War editor of one of the largest national reenactor trade publications.

Living history helped me during a trying time in my life. I became unemployed just after starting our hobby. During this time I had a young family, unemployment was rampant, I went back to college and I was under pressure to find another career. Because of my interest in living history, I chose to study history. This decision led me to get a job with the university museum, which led to museum studies. During my work as curator of history I also took on the job of curator of education. This came in conjunction with making the decision to become a teacher. From that point on my life changed drastically. I not only began my research, but also developed my living history groundwork, my dedication to teaching through our hobby and my quest to link every part of my life to history.

But this portal, this window that I can slip into on the weekends, allows me to put on a fine golden trimmed woolen uniform and don the trappings of authority as a member of the landed gentry and an officer of Massachusetts Bay. This gives me a release valve from reality, which so many of us need. I am able to engross myself in the morality, simplicity and thought of a valiant and honorable time. It was a time when a man's honor was reflected in his personal surroundings, his family and his own fortitude.

As my historic counterparts were able to change their environment, reenacting has given me the same opportunity to change and enhance my life through hard work, dedication and honor. For this I am truly thankful and dedicate my life.

Now you know *too* much about us. But that is one of the nice things about this hobby: that you'll learn so much about each other. For us it has been a wonderful family experience and has fostered a fabulous family of good friends as well. That, we believe, is one of the key elements that you can expect from reenacting.

This doesn't mean you won't have some rapids to paddle, mountains to climb or battles to win, it *is* real life even though you get to slip back in time for the weekends. We hope you can learn from our experiences and ideas and blend them with your own unique portrayals when you become one of us. If you already are a reenactor or living historian, we hope you'll think about some of the ideas we have offered and see how they fit with your portrayals.

It's your choice:

Will you make the commitment?

APPENDIX 1
Useful Web Sites for Reenactors

General:

http://dir.yahoo.com/Arts/Humanities/History/
 U S History/Museums and Memorials/
 National Historic Sites and Landmarks/

http://sg.dir.yahoo.com/Arts/Humanities/History/
 U S History/
 Museums and Memorials/Living History/

Multi-Era:

http://www.reenactor.net/index.htm

http://www.widomaker.com/ ~ poirier/Links.htm

Roman:

http://www.larp.com/legioxx/groups.html

French & Indian War:

http://members.aol.com/fiwar/directory.html

American Revolution:

http://www.revwar.com/links/

War of 1812:

http://www.militaryheritage.com/1812.htm

http://www.cia-g.com/~rockets/domagala.1812.htm

Civil War:

http://sg.dir.yahoo.com/Arts/Humanities/History/
    U_S__History/By_Time_Period/19th_Century/
    Military_History/Civil_War__1861_1865_/Museums_and
    _Memorials/

http://www2.tsixroads.com/~rodbond/
    CW02.html#anchor166710

http://www.cwreenactors.com/

Old West, 19th Century:

http://www.oldwest.org/cows/links.html

Spanish American War:

http://www.saw1898.com/

WWII:

http://www.io.com/~tog/

http://www.alltel.net/~shawkids/wwii/

Korean War & Vietnam:

http://www.reenactor.net/main_htmls/korea_nam.html

Sutlers:

http://members.aol.com/canaltwo/sutlers.htm

http://home.inreach.com/mavgw/sutlers.htm

http://sutlers.freeservers.com/

Funny page, "You know you're a reenactor when..."
http://www.gwerin.org.uk/signs_that_you.htm

APPENDIX 2
Books, Publications, Magazines For Living History

This is not intended to be an all-inclusive list, but rather a starting point for you to look for information and ideas.

Albion's Seed: Four British Folkways in America, David Hackett Fischer, Oxford University Press, Inc., 1991.

Book of Buckskinning, William H. Scurlock (editor), Scurlock Publishing, Inc., 1983.
Book of Buckskinning II, William H. Scurlock (editor), Scurlock Publishing, Inc., 1983.
Book of Buckskinning III, William H. Scurlock (editor), Scurlock Publishing, Inc., 1984.
Book of Buckskinning IV, William H. Scurlock (editor), Scurlock Publishing, Inc., 1987.
Book of Buckskinning V, William H. Scurlock (editor), Scurlock Publishing, Inc., 1989.
Book of Buckskinning VI, William H. Scurlock (editor), Scurlock Publishing, Inc., 1992.
Book of Buckskinning VII, William H. Scurlock (editor), Scurlock Publishing, Inc., 1995.

Interpreting Our Heritage, Freeman Tilden, University of North Carolina Press, 1957.

Living History: Drawing from the Past, Cathy Johnson, Graphics-Fine Arts Press, 1994.

Who Was I? Cathy Johnson, Graphics-Fine Arts Press, 1995.

Past Into Present: Effective Techniques for First-Person Historical Interpretation, Stacy Roth, University of North Carolina Press, 1998.

Time Machine: The World of Living History, Jay Anderson, The American Association for State and Local History, 1984.

— 〰〰〰 —

Muzzle Blasts magazine, NMLRA, PO Box 67, Friendship, IN 47021-0067.
http://ezines.firelands.net/MuzzleBlastsOnline/Vol2No2/

Muzzleloader magazine, Scurlock Publishing, Rt 5, Box 347-M Texarkana, TX. 75501, (903) 832-4726
www.muzzmag.com

On The Trail magazine, Rt. 6, Box 554, Macon, GA 31217 (478) 738-9669. www.ottmagazine.com

Smoke & Fire News, PO Box 166, Grand Rapids, OH 43522, (800) 766-5334, www.smoke-fire.com

APPENDIX 3
Primary Source Record Sheet

Research Library:_____

Title or Name: _____

Author or Editor: _____

Publisher or Co.: _____

Copyright: _____Pages: _____

Original: _____Notes: _____Photocopy_____

Another, name: _____Notes: _____

Place and Date Acquired: _____

Comments: _____

_____

Subjects or Areas of Interest: _____

_____

APPENDIX 4
Military Service Record Sheet

Name: _____

Rank: _____

Unit: _____

Years of Service: _____

Places Served: _____

Commander: _____

Battles: _____

Forts Stationed: _____

Archive Holding Papers: _____

Comments: _____

_____

_____

_____

_____

_____

_____

_____

_____

APPENDIX 5
Sutler / Merchant List

Bradley Company of the Fox
4330 N State Rd 110
Oshkosh, WI 54904
(920) 233-5332
www.bradleycompanyofthefox.com

C & D Jarnagin Co. (1750-1865)
PO Box 1860
Corinth, MS 38834
(662) 287-4977
www.jarnaginco.com

Carl Dyer Moccasins
PO Box 31
Friendship, IN 47021
www.byrge.com/carl dyer moccasins.htm

Dixie Gun Works
Gunpowder Ln
PO Box 130
Union City, TN 38281
1-800-238-6785
www.dixiegunworks.com

Goose Bay Workshops
990 Greenwood Rd
Crozet, VA 22932
(540) 456-6990
www.teleport.com/ ~ walking/goosebay

Castle Keep, Ltd.
83 South LaSalle St
Aurora, IL 60505
Phone 630.801.1696
www.reenact.com

Druid's Oak
11601 Ziegler Rd SE
Hancock, MD 21750
(301) 478-3200

The Emporium
Rt 1, Box 363
Ava, MO 65608
(417) 683-2764

Fugawee Corporation
3127 Corrib Dr
Tallahassee, FL 32308
1-800-749-0387
www.fugawee.com

Heavy Metal Traders
4 So. Western Ave
Aurora, IL 60506
(630) 892-2176

Jas. Townsend & Son, Inc.
PO Box 415-SF
Pierceton, IN 46562
www.jastown.com

Log Cabin Shop
8010 Lafayette Rd., PO Box 275
Lodi, OH 44254
(330) 948-1082
www.logcabinshop.com

The Pillaged Village
274 Cora Dr
Carlisle, OH 45005
www.pillagedvillage.com

Smiling Fox Forge
3500 Co Rd 234
Fremont, OH 43420
(419) 334-8180
www.smilingfoxforge.com

Re-enactment Eyewear
1738 E. Third St #346
Williamsport, PA 17701
(570) 322-9849

The Tin Shop
2014 S. Smithville Rd.
Dayton, OH 45420
(937) 252-9644

Red Hawk Traders
6035 19 Mile Rd
Cedar Spr, MI 49319
(616) 696-3266

Smoke & Fire Co.
PO Box 166
Grand Rapids, OH
43522
(419) 878-8535
www.smoke-fire.com

TENTS:

Four Seasons Tentmasters
4221 Livesay Rd
Sand Creek, MI 49279
(517) 436-6245

Panther Primitives
P.O. Box 32-D
Normantown, WV 25267
(304) 462-7718
www.pantherprimitives.com

R.K. Lodges
Box 567
Hector, MN 55342
(320) 848-6363
www.RKLodges.com

APPENDIX 6
Military Persona Development Worksheet

Civilian Demographics:

Name _____

Ethnic background _____

Language(s) _____

Age _____ Date & place of birth _____

Father _____ Mother _____

Father's occupation _____

Mother's occupation (if applicable) _____

Brothers & Sisters _____

_____

Spouse _____ Marriage date _____

Spouse's family background _____

Children _____

_____

Residence _____ Years _____

Neighbors _____

Education _____ Literate (yes or no) _____

Religion _____ Occupation _____

Special skills _____

Wages _____ Other income _____

Military Service:

Military service dates _____

Unit (s) _____

Commander (s) _____

Expedition (s) _____

Rank(s) _____

Training _____

Battles _____

Wounds _____

Citations _____

APPENDIX 7
SAMPLE:
Small Military Event Schedule

Saturday
9:00 Opening colors
      ceremony
10:00 Demonstration
11:00 Clothing talk
12:00 Lunch
1:00 Demonstration
2:00 Tactical
3:00 Demonstration
5:00 Close to public

Sunday
9:00 Colors ceremony
9:30 Church service
10:00 Demonstration
11:00 Clothing talk
12:00 Lunch
1:00 Demonstration
2:00 Tactical
3:00 Closing ceremony

APPENDIX 8
SAMPLE:
Large Military Event Schedule

Saturday

7:00	Reveille, kindle fires
7:30	N.C.O. Call
7:45	Wood and water call
8:00	Morning Roast Beef (breakfast)
8:30	Officers' Call
9:30	Assembly and inspection
10:00	Colors ceremony
11:00	Firing demonstration
11:45	Wood and water call
12:00	Roast Beef (lunch)
1:00	Uniforms talk
2:00	Cannon demonstration
2:45	Assembly and inspection
3:00	Tactical
4:00	Ladies clothing talk
5:00	Wood and water call
5:30	Roast Beef (dinner)
6:30	Evening assembly and inspection
7:15	Assembly and inspection
8:00	
10:00	Tattoo (restricted to camp)

Sunday

7:00	Reveille, kindle fires
7:30	N.C.O. Call
7:45	Wood and water call
8:00	Morning Roast Beef (breakfast)
8:30	Officers' Call
9:30	Assembly and inspection
10:00	Colors ceremony
10:30	Church service
11:00	Firing demonstration
11:45	Wood and water call
12:00	Roast Beef (lunch)
1:00	Uniforms talk
2:00	Cannon demonstration
2:45	Assembly and inspection
3:00	Tactical
3:45	Closing colors ceremony
4:00	Closed to public

APPENDIX 9
Living History Organizations

Medieval Organizations:
Society of Creative Anachronism
AKA: SCA
c/o PO Box 360789
Milpitas, CA 95063
(408) 263-9305

Maryland Medieval Mercenary Militia
PO Box 715
Greenbelt, MD 20768

English Civil War:
English Civil War Society of America
c/o Keith Frye
33 Ridge Rd
Bloomingdale, NJ 07403
(973) 838-1573
kmfrye@carroll.com
www.ecwsa.org

Cavalier Association
46 Fallis Rd
Columbus, OH 43214
(614) 263-0482
73357.3446@compuserve.com

Seven Years' War (French & Indian War):
Forces of Montcalm and Wolfe, Inc.
RR 1 Box 181
Poland, IN 47868

Associators of the French & Indian War
1143 McEwan Ave
Cannonsburg, PA 15317
(412) 745-0603

The British Military Family, The Organization of British and
    Allied Living History Forces of Michigan
6685 W Nestel Rd
Houghton Lake, MI 48629
(517) 366-6531
kemmerc@k2.kirtland.cc.mi.us

French and Indian War Era Grand Encampment
    Confederation
Brenton C. Kemmer kemmerc@k2.kirtland.cc.mi.us or
Bill Protz protz@dellnet.com

Alliance de La Nouvelle-France
265 E. Wood St
Shreve, OH 44676
(330) 567-2124
ajg153@aol.com

Seven Years' War, England:
8 Warren Court
Underdown Rd
Southwick, Sussex, BN42 4HN UK
(0127) 359-4528

American Revolution:
The Brigade of the American Revolution
531 Westwood Ave
River Vale, NJ 07675
(888) go revwar
www.brigade.org

The Northwest Territory Alliance
W 69 N 358 Evergreen Blvd
Cedarburg, WI 53012
(414) 377-8029
www.nwta.com

The Society of the 18th Century Reenactors
(Midwest only)
27027 Terrel
Dearborn Hts, MI 48127

The Continental Line
154 S Broad St, 1st Floor
Landsdale, PA 19446
(215) 362-7790
CLAdjutant@aol.com

Burning of the Valleys Military Association
Box 657 Kings Highway
Saugerties, NY 12477
(914) 246-6305
www.bvma.org

War of 1812:
North America British Brigade
5538 S Miro St
New Orleans, LA 70125
britcomhmp@aol.com
http://hometown.aol.com/ninety3rd/NAB.html

Brigade Napoleon
18914 Walnut Rd
Castor Valley, CA 94546
www.brigadepub.com/napoleon.html

American Civil War:
Signal Corps Association
www.civilwarsignals.org

North-South Skirmish Association, Inc.
PO Box 361
Bloomfield Hills, MI 48303
www.n-ssa.org

National Civil War Association
PO Box 70084
Sunnyvale, CA 94086
www.ncwa.org

Native American:
National Native American Co-op
PO Box 1000
San Carlos, AZ 85550

Tecumseh Lodge
15160 Cherry Tree
Noblesville, IN 46060

Grand Rapids Inter-Tribal Center
45 Lexington, NW
Grand Rapids, MI 49504

Buckskinning:
National Muzzleloading Rifle Association
PO Box 67
Friendship, IN 47621
(800) 745-1493
www.nmlra.org

The American Mountainman Association
16630 Penny Ave
Sand Lake, MI 49364

Trekking:
Coalition of Historical Trekkers
38901 No Joyce Ave.
Beach Park IL 60099
www.coht.org

APPENDIX 10

Addresses of Historical Sites Mentioned in this Book

American Antiquarian Society
185 Salisbury Street
Worcester, Massachusetts 01609
508-755-5221
http://www.americanantiquarian.org/

Colonial Michilimackinac
Mackinac State Historic Parks
P.O. Box 370
Mackinac Island, MI 49757-0370
Summer (906) 847-3328
Winter 231-436-4100 or 517-373-4296
http://www.mackinac.com/historicparks/index.html

Colonial Williamsburg
Colonial Williamsburg Foundation
P.O. Box 1776
Williamsburg, VA 23187-1776
800-HISTORY
http://www.history.org/

Conner's Prairie
13400 Allisonville Road
Fishers, IN 46038-4499
800-966-1836
http://www.connerprairie.org/

Cultural and Natural History Museum
829 103 Rowe Hall
Central Michigan University
Mt. Pleasant, Michigan 48859
(517) 774-3829
http://www.museum.cmich.edu/

Fort Crown Point
Crown Point State Historic Site
RD 1, Box 219
Crown Point, NY 12928
(518)597-3666
http://cahpwww.nbc.upenn.edu/~thomsen/forts/crown_point.html

Herkimer Home (Fort Herkimer) State Historical Site
200 State Route 169
Little Falls, NY 13365
(315) 823 0398
http://www.littlefallsny.com/HerkimerHome/Page1.htm

Old Fort Johnson
Montgomery County Historical Society
Fort Johnson, NY 12070
518-843-0300

Fort Meigs
29100 West River Road
Perrysburg, OH 43552
419-874-4121 or 800-283-8916
http://www.ohiohistory.org/places/ftmeigs/

Fort Stanwix
112 E. Park St
Rome, NY 13440
315-336-2090
http://www.nps.gov/fost/

Fort Ticonderoga
PO Box 390
Ticonderoga, NY 12883
518-585-2821
http://www.fort-ticonderoga.org

Fort William Henry
Fort William Henry Corporation
48 Canada Street
Lake George, NY 12845
(518) 668-3081, Fax: (518) 668-4926
http://www.fortwilliamhenry.com/fortmus.htm

Johnson Hall
Hall Ave
Johnstown, NY
518-762-8712
http://www.johnstown.com/city/johnson.html

Lake Champlain Maritime Museum
4472 Basin Harbor Rd
Vergennes, VT 05491
802-475-2022, Fax: 802-475-2953
http://www.lcmm.org/

Old Fort Niagara
P.O. Box 169
Youngstown, NY 14174-0169
(716) 745-7611
http://www.oldfortniagara.org/

Plymouth Plantation
P.O. Box 1620
Plymouth, MA 02362
508/746-1622
http://www.plimoth.org/museum/museum.htm

INDEX